D0887111

Information Services for Academic Administration

JB Lon Hefferlin

Ellis L. Phillips, Jr.

Jossey-Bass Inc., Publishers
615 Montgomery Street · San Francisco · 1971

INFORMATION SERVICES FOR ACADEMIC ADMINISTRATION
JB Lon Hefferlin and Ellis L. Phillips, Jr.

Library of Congress Catalog Card Number 76-148659

International Standard Book Number ISBN 0-87589-096-2

Manufactured in the United States of America
Composed and printed by York Composition Company, Inc.
Bound by Chas. H. Bohn & Co., Inc.

JACKET DESIGN BY WILLI BAUM, SAN FRANCISCO

FIRST EDITION

Code 7110

The Jossey-Bass Series
in Higher Education

General Editors

JOSEPH AXELROD
*San Francisco State College
and University of California, Berkeley*

MERVIN B. FREEDMAN
*San Francisco State College
and Wright Institute, Berkeley*

For W. H. COWLEY

*scholarly administrator
and administrative scholar*

Preface

$\mathbb{E}$ducation is the biggest business of the nation apart from defense. And higher education has become the fastest growing segment of the national educational complex—in recent years, almost a national preoccupation. As in any growth industry the pace of change is uneven, and the people involved in it can easily lose perspective about developments. In order to aspire to excellence in education they need help through better information about their own institutions and about educational and social change at large.

The Ellis L. Phillips Foundation is one among many

organizations attempting to meet this need. Organized in 1930 by Ellis L. Phillips, the founder and president of the Long Island Lighting Company, the foundation has sought to aid individuals through the improvement of such social institutions as churches and colleges. For example, concerned about the preparation of academic administrators, the board of directors of the foundation in 1962 authorized a program of one-year internships that allowed promising college and university administrators to work with the president or another central administrative officer of a major university. Enlarged with assistance from the Fund for the Advancement of Education and from the Hazen Foundation, the Phillips internship program aided forty-four men and women during its four years of operation; and its concept of academic internships proved so successful that the Ford Foundation underwrote a major similar program through the American Council on Education in 1965.

Since then the interest of the Phillips Foundation in the problems of college and university administration has expanded. In 1968 it considered organizing a center for research in academic administration that would make available on a nonprofit basis to colleges and universities expert advice on their business and financial operations. This center might also collect, organize, and disseminate facts about administrative problems, sponsor conferences and training programs for administrators, and publish books, newsletters, and abstracts on topics of concern to them.

W. H. Cowley, David Jacks Professor of Higher Education, emeritus, of Stanford University, suggested that before planning for the center proceeded further, the foundation should undertake an inventory of the services already available to administrative officers in higher education and should survey a sample of administrators to learn their preferences about these services and their needs for additional aids. This book

Preface

is the result of that recommendation. We discuss the six major media of information for academic administration, describe and evaluate the sources of information in each of these media, and then propose a series of improvements in these services.

We hope this information about information will be of value to college and university administrators, association officials, foundation executives, officers of federal and state agencies, and other participants in or observers of higher education. Moreover, we hope our recommendations will lead to an improved information system open not only to administrators but also to students, faculty members, trustees, parents, alumni, and concerned members of the public.

We are indebted to the several hundred persons who have counseled us thus far in this project. We want especially to thank Peggy Humphreys and Doris Parker for their assistance during the project as the secretaries of the foundation. We will be grateful for whatever corrections of information or reactions to our recommendations we receive as a result of publishing *Information Services for Academic Administration.*

Ithaca, New York   ELLIS L. PHILLIPS, JR.
Berkeley, California   JB LON HEFFERLIN
January 1971

Contents

NEED FOR IMPROVED SERVICES

The condition of information for academic administration is illustrated, analyzed, diagnosed, evaluated, and summarized, and a meta-information network of information about information is suggested as a partial solution.

Contents

CURRENT AND PROPOSED SERVICES

Contents

Contents

now open to written or telephonic inquiry, and a proposal for making their services widely available by creating a coordinating device for them: a referral service to existing sources of knowledge and expertise about higher education.

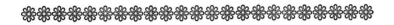

INFORMATION SERVICES
FOR ACADEMIC
ADMINISTRATION

1

Problems of Information

College and university administration as we have come to know it in the United States is now a century old. Before 1870, academic administration was a part-time avocation; since then it has been growing into a profession. In February 1870, Charles W. Eliot, the driving young president of Harvard University, appointed Ephraim W. Gurney as dean of Harvard College to handle all of its problems of student discipline. Eliot was going to concern himself entirely with the organization and effectiveness of the university at large. He was not going to be a disciplinarian or a side-tracked professor, but a full-time leader. Gurney thus became the first real student personnel officer in American higher education, and Eliot the first real executive.[1]

The centennial of administrative division of labor in higher education has not been a time of celebration. During 1970, academic administrators were under attack; academic organization was in disarray; academic government was in turmoil. College presidents, trying to keep coherence among the elements of increasingly centrifugal organizations, found their responsibilities often outpaced their authority. Expanding departments and divisions were expecting expanded autonomy. More constituents were demanding greater voice. And the growth of most institutions required more and more division of labor, bringing with it the attendant problems of bureaucracy and ritualism. Operating procedures seemed to harden into rigid policies, while major policies were enunciated but never implemented in practice. As a result, administrative operations were close to foundering.

One reason for these administrative troubles lies in inadequate information and communication. Without communication, coordination is impossible; without information, institutions are inconceivable. And with the growth of colleges and universities into huge organizations, their need for information and communication has become urgent. Their governing bodies and administrative officers at all levels are no longer able to base decisions on first-hand experience as Eliot and Gurney did when Harvard enrolled only 570 under-

---

[1] See W. H. Cowley, *An Overview of American Colleges and Universities* (Palo Alto, Calif.: Stanford University, 1961), p. 279 (mimeo.).

graduates. Not only do they need facts about their own institutions that are difficult to gain; they also need information about developments and conditions in other institutions, in the community, and in society at large in order to operate effectively.

Consider some problems involving information:

A major state university is receiving an average of three to four bomb threats a day. Its administrative officers have devised some tactics to handle these threats but they wonder whether other institutions have developed better techniques of dealing with the problem. Who is knowledgeable that they should contact?

Another state university has constructed buildings and assigned them to departments without bothering to examine their utilization. The university runs into difficulties when the state legislature conducts its own space-utilization study and finds that the university is using its facilities less efficiently than any other public college or university in the state.

The policy-making bodies of a debt-ridden university, struggling to balance its budget, do not have access to the fact that 40 per cent of its classes enroll only ten or fewer students.

A faculty committee at a state university is considering the adoption of pass-fail grading and wonders about its effects at other institutions. They ask if any evaluations have been made elsewhere, but they do not know where to find out.

The provost of a new state college in a state capital is interested in opening a master's program in public administration. He wonders what institutions are doing creative things in this field—but he does not know whom to ask.

A five-day workshop for college administrators

3

is being devoted to the latest developments in planning, programming, and budgeting systems. Not until the fourth day of the workshop does its staff learn through a show of hands of the participants that thirty of the hundred institutions represented at the sessions do not even operate with budgets.

The newly-appointed staff director for a university self-study has to take time off to fly to other institutions currently engaged in self-studies in order to learn how to conduct one, because he cannot locate anyone with broad knowledge about self-studies. "It was a damned expensive education," he reports.

A college president is bemoaning the sessions of a national conference. "Here we are still talking about the goals of American higher education, and I need practical sessions on things like injunctions and what, if anything, to do about homosexual faculty members."

An administrator at an Ivy League university says that the reading matter coming into his office daily was a brief case full a year ago. Now it is a suitcase full.

These cases illustrate the problem of administrative information in higher education. On the one hand college officials are swamped with snippets of seemingly useless data, and on the other they often lack the information they need to be effective in their work. Deluged with memoranda, reports, publications, and advice, detained by one meeting or discussion from beginning another, they sense themselves ill-informed about the problems on which they must act. Moreover, many students, professors, and staff members are poorly informed about their institutions. And worst of all, even more of them feel that they are uninformed—and consequently that they are victimized, powerless institutional pawns. When administrators believe they lack useful information in the midst

4

of seemingly useless data, while at the same time other participants in higher education sense that they lack access even to these data, remedy is necessary.

We believe that the channels of information useful for determining and carrying out policy in higher education are both overburdened and underdeveloped. Strengthening these channels will not solve all the problems of beleaguered academic administrators and benighted academic institutions, but it can help avoid some of their disasters.

A dual problem exists: Most informal communication channels are unavoidably parochial, and most formal channels are so unnecessarily impersonal as to be unresponsive. Talk is constrained; print is rampant. To be specific, informal communication (the shop-talk among friends and colleagues, the chance meetings over coffee and at conferences, the phone calls to keep tuned in on the grapevine) by its very nature is unsystematic. Some institutions, just as some individuals, are plugged into knowledgeable informal networks: their members circulate in the right company. Their administrators have prestige; their professors, renown; their trustees, contacts. They have entree to knowledge. But other institutions do not. They remain on the periphery of knowledge: needing help but lacking information about how to get it. Thus the neediest college may typically end up with the least competent counsel. "What do you do?" asks one administrator. "You call a friend who knows a friend who knows a self-defined expert." As a result, the blind lead the blind. Or the institution simply makes do without information. For example, a small church-related college in Ohio recently had the opportunity to reorganize its student personnel services, and its president wondered how other colleges of similar size had organized theirs. "We do not know whether such information is available," he admitted, "and if it is, where to find it."

Moreover, specialists specialize. Their duties separate

them from other specialists. Administrators commiserate with administrators, scholars communicate with scholars, students rap with students. The scholar may have facts important for administration, but the administrator may not know of them —or trust them. More often, when an administrator turns to the scholar for advice the scholar is ill-prepared to advise. His data are not complete; they are not problem oriented; they do not bear on practice. Thus the gulf between administrator and scholar remains unbridged. What is more, the researchers specializing in the study of higher education from a variety of backgrounds have only sporadic communication with each other.

In short, most informal channels of communication are short, narrow, and rutted. And on the formal level, communication channels are inefficient. They are mass oriented rather than individualized: they are *producer planned* rather than *consumer stimulated*. They consist in the broadcast dissemination of data through newsletters, journals, and mass mailings ground out by institutions, associations, and agencies, rather than in specific individually-initiated assistance.

A consumer-stimulated information system would provide assistance as needed on the request of the user. But a producer-planned system operates on an inflexible schedule. If disseminated data are not useful when distributed, they must be catalogued, stored, remembered, and then retrieved at an appropriate time in the future. It is as if the United States Department of Agriculture sent to every household in the nation brochures on attacking the boll weevil in hopes that some families would benefit from them.

Unfortunately for producer-planned systems, *data are not information*. Data have information potential, but they do not by themselves constitute information. The recipient alone decides if a bit of data is information by deciding if it is relevant to his needs. Unless it informs, unless it changes his

6

knowledge and ideas, it is not information. Higher education thus suffers from a plethora of data systems and a paucity of information systems. Its formal channels of communication are heavily unidirectional. Questionnaires are distributed en masse by people with time to spare to those who lack time; and if the resulting data are ever assembled for the benefit of the cooperating individuals, they are produced for officials or institutions as a group rather than being made available to individual administrators, faculty members, students, or trustees. Despite the glut of disseminating devices, individuals lack the opportunities for inquiry, consultation, and conversation that provide significant information when they want and can use it.

The Educational Resources Information Center (ERIC) is a case in point. Touted by the United States Office of Education as a "national information system" for collecting, storing, and distributing information on education, ERIC and its contract clearinghouses limit themselves to the literature of education and to publishing facts about this literature—not to answering inquiries about expertise and knowledge within education. Helpful as in part it is, the ERIC system is ponderously inadequate. ERIC is not a national information system: it is a national bibliographic system.

No producer-planned information service, such as ERIC or the others listed in the later chapters of this report, can by themselves meet the need of administrators for knowledge. Consumer-stimulated inquiry and consultation services must be expanded. But the simple expansion of existing services will still not meet the need. The most urgent improvement in information services for academic administration is the creation of a higher level of information service than now exists: a level that some specialists in information theory have come to call *meta*information. Metainformation means information *about* information—information about where information exists and where knowledge can be found. More than anything else, higher education administration requires better metainformation: a means by which all the members of the academic community can be informed about information and knowledgeable about knowledge in higher education.

The first priority of any information system is to know the existing sources of information—to know where data exist, to identify the location of expertise, and to be able to refer inquirers to these sources. Just as libraries have reference shelves and desks, legislatures have legislative reference services, health agencies have poison information centers and suicide prevention services, and the scientific community has the National Referral Center for Science and Technology, now the system of American higher education needs a hot-line system of information about information.

Among the labels for such a system could be these: *people bank; inquiry service; information exchange; talent pool; switchboard service; reference and referral service.* Such an information center would not need to supersede any of the presently diverse and specialized centers of knowledge about higher education, such as the individual scholars and experts, the university programs, the association officers, and the government agencies concerned with college education. Instead it should be a coordinating agent for them. To these sources of knowledge it should bring the problems raised by faculty, students, administrators, trustees, officials, and interested members of the public—the university administrator dealing with bomb threats, the institution concerned with space utilization, the faculty committee curious about evaluations of pass-fail grading, the provost interested in public administration programs, the self-study director seeking experience, the president wondering about the structure of student personnel.

Already, of course, some knowledgeable people in certain positions within universities, foundations, associations, and government devote much effort informally in putting others in touch with sources of information; and some of them in the know rather enjoy their exclusive franchise. Their efforts would be more useful if expanded, systematized, and democratized. Thus we urge the development of consumer-stimulated sources of higher educational knowledge into a system that brings the inquirer and the information together. Without such a system, data and knowledge will continue to be under-utilized while inquiry remains inefficient. Without such a service, higher education will not escape the condition that Harold Wilensky observes elsewhere: "In every sphere of modern life, the chronic condition is a surfeit of information, poorly integrated or lost somewhere in the system."[2]

In brief, the information system that we advocate operates on the basic educational principle of helping people learn how they can obtain knowledge and assistance for themselves. We support improvements in all of the existing sources of administrative information described in later chapters. But beyond these several media we advocate their coordination through the creation somewhere within the community of higher education of a higher education information center: a people bank which does not presume to contain all the facts about colleges and universities as would a massive data bank, but which instead serves as a resource to information and expertise elsewhere—in sum, as a metainformation device.

[2] H. L. Wilensky, "Organizational Intelligence," *International Encyclopedia of the Social Sciences* (New York: Macmillan Company and The Free Press, 1968), vol. 11, p. 331.

2

Demand for
Information

"Administrators don't need information," says
Peter Schrag, a former editor of *Change* and *Saturday Review*. "They need a good kick in the pants." As he and some
other observers see it, the central problem of academic administration is not a lack of information but a lack of compassion and action. In illustrating his concern, Schrag commented to us, "Whenever an administrator hears a complaint

about an ineffective professor and says to himself, 'Well, he's only got three more years until retirement,' and doesn't do anything about it, he's stopped being concerned with the education of students and is concerned instead with the preservation of the institution."

Certainly it is true that many of the present problems of academic institutions do not stem primarily from a lack of information. At any number of colleges and universities, for instance, the decentralization of power is long overdue. Administrative offices must become responsive, accountable, effective. Their practices need to be brought into line with policy. But even in these problem areas, information is needed: facts about the techniques of change, about alternative solutions, about good practice. When a president or provost is so isolated that he hears no complaints about bad teaching, when he is not able to be acquainted with the individuals involved, when he knows no means to reduce the persistent problem of deadwood, then problems of information do exist and require action. Without access to knowledge, in short, effective decisions are unlikely. Instead, they may be inept, unwitting, misguided, unwise, inadequate, and irresponsible. The trustees of a college may have to disagree with the majority of its students over the issue of tuition increase, but they would be foolhardy to act without any reference to student attitudes. And since it is desirable for an institution to plan alternatives to its practice of shutting down its computer every day at five in the afternoon, it is essential for the administrators of the institution to realize that the computer center does close at five.

Some administrators in higher education readily admit the problems that inadequate information can cause. For example, Lyman Glenny, formerly the executive director of the Illinois Board of Higher Education and now at Berkeley, said to us, "I was frustrated in Illinois because I didn't have the information I needed in usable form, and yet I suspected it existed somewhere. But did it exist—and where was it? Someone would remember that they had seen some facts in one of the sociological journals within the past couple years, but they couldn't recall anything more specific than that." And James Perkins, former president of Cornell, reflecting on Cornell's need for information in its decision making, states, "The biggest barrier at Cornell was that the data were buried. It was like having oil four hundred feet underground and no way of getting to it. It was useless."

For most administrators, however, the issue of adequate information is not high on their list of problems. Their most pressing difficulties, as several surveys have shown, are typically first financial, then political and governmental, sometimes interpersonal, and only occasionally educational. The problem of access to needed information seems to be at a lower level for most of them: a level of persistent, chronic problems such as one's own physical stamina, the allocation of time, and the adequacy of the administrative staff. All of these conditions affect the solution of financial, political, and educational problems, but administrators tend to view them as secondary.

In regard to their problems of information, most presidents and deans with whom we have corresponded tell us that their worst difficulty is in fact not the lack of useful information but instead the oppression of useless data. Their annoyance and frustration over unwanted facts are virtually universal. Professors may believe that administrative conspiracies prevent the faculty from getting access to institutional facts; students may resent their own lack of knowledge about institutional policies and practices; office staff members may be demoralized because of inadequate communication; the governing board may believe itself patronized by insufficient information; but administrators feel inundated.

12

Demand for Information

Listen to this litany from the administrators with whom we talked and corresponded for this report:

I fear we suffer badly from information overload.

The field is overcrowded as it is. . . . The average academic administrator is already getting far more information than he has the time to read or assimilate.

The central problem is one of digesting what we get.

Administrators don't need more information, they need a better set of inner and outer systems of communication.

There is much too much printed matter coming across the desk of everyone. What is probably needed most is a system of having it boiled down.

Throughout these and similar complaints runs an objection not only to useless data but also to reading as the means of learning. Although printing is a cheap means of distributing facts, reading is a slow way of learning them for a busy administrator. Even if by temperament and training an administrator is visually minded, he is typically forced by circumstances to become aurally tuned. Whether by conversing in the office, picking up the phone, or journeying to the necessary location, he prefers getting information directly when it is needed. (A study of the use of college presidents' time as logged by their secretaries illustrates this fact. For better or worse, the presidents studied spend three-fourths of their office days in group meetings and individual conferences, and only 3.9 per cent in reading and reflection.[1])

[1] J. K. Hemphill and H. J. Walberg, "An Empirical Study

13

Information Services for Academic Administration

In summary, the only virtually unanimous opinion we have obtained from administrators about improving administrative information can be phrased simply as *not more publications, but improved publications*—more succinct and more substantial. Aside from having this one widespread complaint about publications, the administrators with whom we have discussed the problem of information do not agree among themselves about other needed improvements. No particular problem or area of concern receives majority support; no one device or medium of communication is considered uniquely helpful. As part of this project, we asked nearly 130 academic administrators for their suggestions about information services, and we received reactions from seventy-nine of them. Among the diverse subjects on which they report wanting information, two appear more regularly than any others.

One is that of improving their personal effectiveness. An administrator at an eastern women's college put it well:

> *The universal problem, I suppose, is one of too little time for the tasks that have to be done and the effect that this condition causes, namely a constant requirement to react rather than act. Contesting this situation daily, I continually wonder if there are more efficient and effective ways to administer what I do, and where do I find out? This question covers everything from file systems to personnel to office organization and equipment to communication. . . . My suggestion, . . . then, is to establish a service or services to help educational administrators professionalize their institution's administrative organization and their own practice of administration through the*

of College and University Presidents in the State of New York," in *College and University Presidents: Recommendations and Report of a Survey.* New York State Regents Advisory Committee on Educational Leadership (Albany: New York State Department of Education, n.d.).

Demand for Information

*application of the most contemporary procedures and
philosophies of management.*

Similar questions are being asked by other administrators: How can you decide on priority areas for your time and energy? How can you evaluate yourself and compensate for your own weaknesses, as in fiscal matters? How to delegate operating responsibilities in order to provide direction for the institution? These are personal skills in which college officials seek improvement.

A second area of wide concern beyond their personal development is that of administrative structure. "The organization of authority on many campuses is ragged, out-of-date, or inept," the sociologist Bernard Barber has said. "And the ranks of the administration are woefully thin, considering the rapidly expanding work load that universities are being asked to undertake."[2] How best correct such weaknesses? How coordinate responsibilities? How educate new administrative colleagues, such as department chairmen, to their duties, since they seldom meet with one another to discuss their common roles and responsibilities? And how prevent stagnation within middle-management ranks and in nonacademic offices, where officials increasingly feel themselves trapped in dead-end jobs and bureaucratic routine?

Beyond these two areas the needs for information are scattered endlessly, from facts about federal funding to developments in library technology and from trends in teaching loads to the utility of program budgeting. How should we adapt the Philadelphia Plan in hiring minority construction workers? What system of faculty government seems more effective for a faculty of two hundred? What are our students

[2] B. Barber, "Professors, Authority, and Change," *Columbia College Today,* 1967–1968, *15* (2), 40.

learning? What is the likely need for higher education in our region? The permutations of inquiry are infinite. And where can administrators seek this information? If not in the back issues of the *Educational Record, Liberal Education,* and ERIC's *Research in Education,* then where? Here again, our informants advocate the improvement of no one medium of assistance. Some suggest improved communication within their institutions through reliance on home-grown expertise and increased institutional research. Others advocate external aids: opportunities to communicate with neighboring institutions, cooperative inter-institutional research, workshops and institutes, consultation services, access to information and expertise elsewhere. But none of these devices was mentioned by more than a fifth of the administrators we queried. Instead they each received mention by a handful of administrators in this proportion: [3]

	Per Cent
Communication within the institution	14
Informal communication with colleagues elsewhere	15
Cooperative interinstitutional research	10
Institutes and workshops	14
Abstracts and bibliographies	15
Consultation services	18
Access to an information center	14

Thus we are led to believe that efforts to improve information services for college and university administration cannot be limited to any one medium—not even to the meta-information center which we advocate as of central importance. Not only must publications be improved, but the

[3] Percentage of responses from seventy-nine administrators to a written request for advice about information services "that you need—either for yourself, your staff, or leaders in the faculty or on the board."

16

other channels of information listed above and described in the following chapters must be strengthened.

Improvements in these sources of information should help reduce some of the problems that now afflict American higher education and should permit colleges and universities to become more effective. Often not enough information will be available for people to make the best decisions, but better information will enable even the most experienced individuals to make better decisions.

3

Internal
Campus
Communication

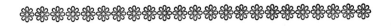

During 1970, a close observer of Columbia University was talking about its difficulties of the past several years. "Columbia's problem is not structural," he maintained. "It is basically a simple lack of information. President Kirk wasn't able to know what was going on. Cordier wasn't able to. And the board to this day doesn't know what's happening." Columbia's recent problems are not unique. An assistant chancellor at a midwestern state university says "more than nationally-available materials and assistance, our need is mostly at an institutional level right here in terms of data gathering and institutional studies capacity." A dean of a graduate school of business comments, "When you walk outside the business school you feel you're in an insane asylum, things are run so badly." And outside consultants agree. Richard Paget, a founder of Cresap, McCormick and Paget, Inc., has said this about colleges and universities surveyed by the firm:

> *It is regularly a finding of our consulting studies that managers of institutions simply do not have the data they need to make timely, effective decisions. . . . It is a regrettable fact that most major decisions on commitments of resources, expansion of an institution, or enlargement of programs still are made largely on the basis of intuition rather than systematic factual analysis. . . . Radical improvement in information systems, and in the decision-making process at all staff levels, could be a worthwhile objective for nearly every institution we know about.*[1]

One out of every seven college administrators whom we questioned for this report said that his greatest need for information is not from outside experts or from other colleges but instead is from within his own institution itself. How well is classroom space being used? What should the portfolio of investments be returning? What will be the costs of a program

[1] R. M. Paget, "Management Problems in Educational and Health Institutions," a presentation to the Third International Conference of Management Consultants, New York, October 30, 1969, p. 11 (mimeo.).

in medical technology? Do students want to live in the dormitories? What were the expenses of the institution last year? What educational impact is the institution making?

Sometimes the answers to these questions do not exist: no one knows the facts. Other times the information is trapped somewhere—in inaccessible offices or incompatible files or even on scraps of paper stuck in the copy of the university by-laws kept by the secretary of the governing board. In any event, significant information is unavailable. As a consequence, many institutions have difficulty in planning where they are going, and some have difficulty even knowing where they are. At one such college, the admissions office believes there are 1,200 freshmen; the registrar has records of only eight hundred; and no one can explain, among these eight hundred, the seventy-five who are in fact attending classes but were never admitted.

Half of the problem of inadequate information lies in finding the facts. The other half lies in getting the facts distributed to the right people. Consider these two issues in turn.

INFORMATION GATHERING

Most criticisms of administration-by-hunch-and-by-hope focus on a lack of institutional intelligence—intelligence not in the sense of secret espionage but of knowledge useful in planning: knowledge about the institution, about problems and aspirations of its members, and about its environment; knowledge that permits alternative futures to be forecast and contingencies anticipated.

How can this intelligence be developed? One answer, of course, is through staff members specializing in intelligence: institutional research specialists, operations analysts, offices of analytic studies. These specialists naturally can be helpful, particularly when they assist the entire membership of the institution and not only administrative officers. But they are only a partial and by themselves inadequate solution. Other means can be used as well for gathering and sharing institutional information. Here are six which deserve increased emphasis within higher education:

Listening

The most elemental step in improving internal communication and information remains that of hearing. Who, in essence, within the administration is listening to what is being said? Only the receptionists and secretaries? Only an ombudsman or the counseling staff? This problem has reached major proportions, according to some observers of academic administration. Among them, Morris Keeton, former dean of Antioch and now head of Antioch, Columbia, in Maryland, has been dismayed at the wide discrepancies that he and his research associates have found on many campuses between the problems expressed by students and faculty members and those perceived by department chairmen and central administrators at the same institutions. In some cases, he reports, they seem to be living in different worlds.

Alvin Eurich at the Academy for Educational Development observes that college presidents have been trying to avoid the necessity of talking with students just as forty years ago corporation executives futilely tried to avoid talking with union representatives. And Robert Merry, at the Harvard Business School, recalls an illustration of the ironic consequences of not listening: At one of his institutes for college and university presidents, he introduced a case study of a Latin American university whose students had occupied the administration building. One president dismissed the case by saying, "This is so ridiculous it isn't worth discussing"—only later to find himself in the same predicament.

Information Services for Academic Administration

Improvements in listening require no additional staff but they may demand major reorientations of staff behavior and attitudes. They may involve an open-door policy by the president, a daily staff meeting at half past nine for administrative officers, subventions to faculty members for their expenses in having students home for supper, or even better briefings of the switchboard operators. But they can make the difference between community and conflict.

Using Available Skills

Some institutions fail to employ the existing talents of their members—the ideas of students, the suggestions of staff, the expertise of professors in fields from business administration to landscape architecture, the experience of trustees. Even more colleges fail to develop the competence of their staff members, operating instead on a philosophy of centralized directives and a staffing policy of getting by on the skills of the wives of graduate students and the widows of past professors.

In contrast, institutions can rely on internal competence by organizing task-forces on foreseeable problems, by having faculty members periodically share administrative responsibilities, by rotating tasks among the staff, and by developing in-house consultants. For instance, Sanford Ericksen, at the University of Michigan, provides ready counsel on instruction as director of its Center for Research on Learning and Teaching. Saxton Pope, at Berkeley, has been available for psychological counsel to the staff after having retired as director of the psychiatry department of the health service at the university. And Sharvy Umbeck, president at Knox College, has seen to it that the governing board of Knox is stacked with experts on call for the college. "Our board contains five investment men who realize that they are responsible for investment policy," he told us. "We've got three educators who are concerned with academic affairs. Five management men are charged to be available in this area; we've two public relations men, and three contractors. Now we're asking ourselves whether other competencies aren't needed on the board; and since our construction program is slowing down, whether we'll need this much construction expertise in the future."

On most campuses, the most under-employed experts on information about higher education are probably the reference librarians. Many inquiries that administrators address to Washington, D.C. could quickly be answered by the campus librarian and the *Fact Book on Higher Education*. Progressive institutions are utilizing the resources of their own library staffs. In addition, some are employing faculty expertise by creating offices of institutional research not as isolated and segregated analytic units but instead as agencies to stimulate and help coordinate institutional research undertaken by individuals and officers throughout the campus. And the most enlightened institutions have organized staff development programs, either unilaterally or in cooperation with other agencies such as the Western Interstate Commission for Higher Education or the American Council on Education. Currently, for example, thirty-five colleges and universities are cooperating in the Academic Administration Internship Program of the American Council by nominating a member of their faculty or staff for nine months' participation as an ACE Fellow on their own campus or another. The fellows meet together at ACE expense for two five-day seminars at the beginning and near the end of their internship, and in the interim serve at the expense of their institutions as an administrative participant-observer under the tutelage of the president or another senior administrator.

Information Services for Academic Administration

*For
Information*

*Charles G. Dobbins, Director
Academic Administration
Internship Program
American Council on Education
One Dupont Circle
Washington, D.C. 20036
(202) 833-4762*

Systematic Polling

Above and beyond the preceding techniques, some colleges and universities are developing an additional source of information through regular questionnaire and interview surveys. A few universities have resorted to outside market research firms to obtain frank opinions from students or faculty members about existing problems. A number have developed systematic student evaluations of teaching and periodic surveys of alumni. And many are beginning to use ready-made questionnaires in order to compare the attitudes of their students and faculty with those of students and faculty members nationally. For canvassing faculty opinions, for example, the Educational Testing Service now has available its Institutional Functioning Inventory, containing such evaluative questions as "In reality a small group of individuals tend to pretty much run this institution" and "Planning at this institution is continuous rather than one-shot or completely nonexistent." Among the ready-made instruments for obtaining facts on student opinions are the College Student Questionnaire and the College and University Environment Scales of the Educational Testing Service, the Institutional Self-Study Service Survey of the American College Testing Program, and the Student Information Form of the American Council on Education. (For information on the latter, see page 129.)

Internal Campus Communication

For
Information

Eldon Park, Director
Institutional Research Program
in Higher Education
Educational Testing Service
Princeton, New Jersey 08540
(609) 921-9000

Oscar T. Lenning
Institutional Self-Study Service
American College Testing
Program
Post Office Box 168
Iowa City, Iowa 52240
(319) 351-4470

Developing Usable Records

Most record-keeping in higher education has remained historically-oriented rather than future-oriented. Thus fund accounting in colleges has served its trustee and stewardship purposes—but is now recognized as inadequate for planning in comparison with cost accounting or management accounting on a program basis. Just as the famous Du Pont chart room of management information led by thirty years the development of usable information within American industry, so American industry at large has led American education in using internal records for policy decisions. By simply keeping a running curve of acceptances among freshman applicants during the spring and summer, a college can sense in comparison with previous years whether or not potential enrollment difficulties are developing, rather than waiting until students begin arriving in September.

Usable records form the heart of what are coming to be called management information systems: systems capable of providing reliable information quickly for decision making. Unfortunately most of the recent attention to these systems in higher education has centered on the needs of central administrative officers alone, to the exclusion of other members of the institution. The management of education requires information about instruction and research as well. John A. Hrones, of Case Western Reserve University, has described as well as anyone the breadth of usable information such a system must contain:

> *In its broadest context, a well-designed and implemented administrative information system is needed to provide every teacher with current information which helps realize a better learning situation for every student. The information system also must enable the faculty member to reduce to a minimum the time he spends on paper work. It must provide current information in an easily usable form to those charged with administering departments, schools, and research projects in order to free them of routine and permit more time for the educational development aspects of their work. It must provide the president and his staff with access to a wide variety of factual data regarding people, physical plant, equipment, courses, research projects, and proposed undertakings to help them develop strong planning efforts. And it must make available pertinent information on the consequences of courses of action to facilitate important educational and management decisions.*[2]

The growth of institutional research during the past twenty years has been a step in this direction, but so far few institutions have aimed at the breadth of information system that Hrones and others advocate.

[2] J. A. Hrones, *Feasibility Study and Recommended Plan for Establishing an Institute for Information Systems in Higher Education* (Washington, D.C.: Associated Universities, Inc., 1969), p. II-3.

Information and records systems can aid in decision making by providing a floor for planning and forecasting the consequences of current trends. Most colleges have goals (at least that of survival, let alone education), and data are necessary to attain them. Programs must be organized to accomplish them; resources allocated most usefully; effects and outcomes audited and evaluated. Planning must thus become comprehensive and long-term. More and more major universities and state systems, including the State University of New York, the University of California, and the University of Illinois, have organized systematic planning operations of this type. At Massachusetts Institute of Technology, for example, a small Office of Institutional Studies began operation in 1960 in the registrar's office. By 1967 it was renamed the Office of Administrative Systems and was assigned along with the planning office of MIT to report directly to the vice-president for organization systems; and it has now developed comprehensive data systems on the personnel, plant, and finances of the institute. "The refinement we plan now," Vice-President John Wynne said, "is to push the planning horizon still further ahead to coordinate all these separate elements into a single framework so that, given the interacting systems character of the institute, the effects of decisions in one area on the whole can be evaluated."[3]

Long before planning, programming, and budgeting became a doctrine within the federal government, major university schools of business were preaching its gospel. A few managed to organize their own operations on its philosophy.

[3] J. M. Wynne, Report of the Vice-President, Organization Systems, in "Report of the President," *Massachusetts Institute of Technology Bulletin,* 1968, *104* (3), 758.

27

Information Services for Academic Administration

Now, pushed by federal requirements and state demands, universities at large are at last catching up with their business schools. (The most readable introduction to planning, programming, and budgeting in academia is *Why Planning, Programming, Budgeting Systems for Higher Education?* by James Farmer, available for $1 from the Western Interstate Commission for Higher Education, Post Office Drawer P, Boulder, Colorado 80302.)

Simulation

The most sophisticated information technique now available for educational planning is computerized simulation of the outcomes of possible decisions. One simulation model for higher education was developed by Richard W. Judy and Jack Levine of Toronto in their work for the Commission on the Financing of Higher Education and was dubbed by them as CAMPUS—Comprehensive Analytical Methods for Planning in University Systems (see page 60). A more recent one is the Resource Requirements Prediction Model of the Planning and Management Systems project of the Western Interstate Commission for Higher Education (see page 56). Stemming from the work of George Weathersby, this model is designed to assist in the prediction of resources required to provide instructional services for any projected enrollments, given certain data regarding faculty, staff, facilities, and equipment. These and other computerized models are permitting increasingly realistic simulation because of the number of factors they can include in their analysis.

Training seminars on these simulation techniques are now available to college and university officers, as indicated on pages 56 and 60. Because of the federal and state interest in the WICHE Planning and Management Systems project, its

28

techniques are likely to affect eventually the information-gathering and decision-making procedures of almost all American colleges.

Improvements in information gathering and decision making, however, are not dependent on computers and simulation. They can be achieved by using all of the means listed so far, including simple listening. "Many managers today are making decisions using less than one-tenth of the information that would be available to them without a computer," says John Dearden, the 1970 educational director of the Institute for Educational Management at Harvard.[4] By collecting and organizing data usefully, by encouraging the existing competence of others, by improving budget procedures, academic administrators can solve major information needs on their own.

INFORMATION SHARING

Beyond the need to obtain information some college and university administrators express serious concern about the dissemination of information throughout their institution. Examples of bottlenecks and breakdowns to warrant their concern are legion: the state university whose faculty members rebel at a major innovation in instruction because it is sprung on them without consultation; the college torn apart through secrecy, cliques, and cabals; the private university in turmoil because of ignorance that its South African investments have been dropped.

Administrative theorists state the problem succinctly: "The maximum size of an effective unit is limited by the ability of that unit to solve its problems of internal communica-

[4] J. Dearden, "Can Management Information Be Automated?" *Harvard Business Review*, 1964, *42* (2), 134.

tion."[5] Recently a good number of American universities have appeared to exceed this maximum size. Having originally relied on compulsory chapel as their one medium of communication, and more recently having depended as a successor on the vagaries of the student newspaper, university officials have been outwitted in the past few years by the mimeograph machine, the walkie-talkie, and the bull-horn. Amends are frantically being made. Bulletin boards are being hung; kiosks assembled; representative assemblies elected; newsletters scheduled in which the full texts of campus documents are being published and space is made available for opinions of all shades about on-campus and off-campus issues.

The University of Michigan illustrates the trend in publications. Three years ago the major channels of communication about its activities were the student and Ann Arbor papers. Because of growing faculty resentment over the apparent exclusion of the faculty from university decisions, the administration revamped the biweekly *University Record* into a weekly academic newsletter with multiple copies distributed to all departments of the institution. In 1968 it inaugurated *U-M News,* mailed twice a month to the nonacademic staff, and *Management Intercom* for supervisory personnel. Later that year it introduced *News Brief,* a recorded telephone news message available twenty-four hours a day, updated every afternoon and more frequently during emergencies.

Other institutions have begun similar services and are developing emergency rumor centers in addition. Students at MIT organized such a communications center that operated for three critical days in 1969, using runners to get facts and a telephone room to squelch rumors. Cornell subsequently organized its rumor clinic on a continuing basis as a result of

[5] H. A. Simon, D. W. Smithburg, and V. A. Thompson, *Public Administration* (New York: Knopf, 1950), p. 131.

its own problems; both Yale and Stanford followed suit in 1970; and, after the Kent State incident, Brandeis students did so temporarily on a national level at their student strike information center. Some institutions, such as the University of Texas, have organized telephonic information and counseling services, as illustrated in Chapter Eight. And at hundreds of colleges, reforms are being made in the form and composition of legislative bodies to assure wider participation in policy decisions.

CONCLUSIONS

Communication is imperative for organization. Without it, social organizations cannot function. Like other social institutions, colleges and universities need to keep the right hand knowledgeable about the left. They require systematic means of collecting, organizing, and sharing information. Directories, coffee breaks, newsletters, open houses, bulletin boards, budgets, all can help.

Most of these devices for increasing information and communication can be implemented without outside funding. Some foundation support has been useful for experimental and demonstration projects, such as those underwritten at several universities by the Esso Educational Foundation and the Ford Foundation. But by and large, these improvements require not additional funds but instead reallocation of existing funds and effort. Reallocation may require outside assistance—information about improvements at other institutions, reports of new strategies and tactics, access to training workshops, possibly outside consultation. But above all it demands the example and attention of the college president himself. Of necessity he must exemplify the pattern of communication for the institution. He himself affects its operation more directly than anyone else. Increasingly his is the responsibility for assuring that communication takes place.

Daniel Griffiths, the theorist of educational administration, has observed, "It is not the function of the chief executive to make decisions; it is his function to monitor the decision-making process to make certain that it performs at the optimum level."[6] His theorem can be paraphrased as well to apply to the collection and distribution of institutional information: It is not the function of the chief executive alone to gather and communicate information; it is his function to monitor the communications process to make certain that it too performs at the optimum level.

[6] D. E. Griffiths, *Administrative Theory* (New York: Appleton-Century-Crofts, 1959), p. 89.

4

Communication
Between
Institutions

The editor of *College and University Business,* Dennis Binning, suggests that if a foundation wants to aid college administrators the most it can take one simple step: provide them with telephone credit cards. His idea could help reduce the isolation that many academic administrators feel. A fourth of those whom we questioned mentioned a need to communicate with their colleagues at other institutions by one means or another. "Especially for college presidents there is a constant sense of lonely exposure," one such president told us, "and anything that helped to create a sense of community, even among a few, would be beneficial." Said another, "I am astounded at how much I must operate in a vacuum. . . . Reading of the onslaught of literature that crosses my desk is not a substitute for access to the counsel and advice of men with similar problems."

Beyond the telephone, three means are available to provide this counsel: travel, periodic meetings, and sharing of institutional research data. Consider each of these in turn.

TRAVEL AND TALK

Private conversation remains the primary means for administrators to get privileged information. (The major reason that institutional associations of colleges and universities operate as presidential clubs lies in the opportunity they offer for presidents to level with each other. When deans appear, the presidents depart.) Visits provide an opportunity for relaxed commiseration. In this connection, one administrator advocates one-day or even half-day trips to other campuses for comparing notes. Another recommends week-long visits of administrators as "exchange consultants" to other institutions where they can both learn and advise. A third recommends month-long sabbaticals for administrators to enable them to visit particularly innovative institutions, with grants-in-aid going to the host institutions as recompense for their hospitality. And a more radical observer of academe proposes that college officials visit industrial executives rather than each other in order to learn how large organizations really should be administered.

Only two foundation programs have aimed specifically at providing opportunities such as these. First, from 1939 until 1965 the Carnegie Corporation financed the travel of two or three potential administrators each year for a period of between two and four months. Until last year Carnegie also supported a similar program for foreign travel of a few well-established presidents each year.

Second, since 1968 the Danforth Foundation has set aside $100 thousand annually for a short-term leave grants program in which it has invited twenty presidents a year (with three of the twenty from two-year colleges) to take several months for travel. Danforth has undertaken the project simply on a demonstration basis in order to convince institutions of the value of administrative leaves that are comparable to faculty sabbaticals and in hopes that they will adopt the idea themselves.

Administrative leaves such as these begun by Carnegie and Danforth deserve wide-spread imitation by institutions. In addition, institutions should budget funds for shorter, more frequent trips as well—not simply for the president but for any representative whose travel is likely to benefit the institution.

PERIODIC MEETINGS

One midwestern college president of our acquaintance tries to visit Santa Cruz at least twice a year to learn as much as possible about the development of the University of California there. His continuing interest in its progress and its innovations for application back home illustrates the need not only for single visits to other campuses but for repeated meetings with colleagues from them. One means for recurring administrative interchange is through consortia—for example, the Great Lakes Colleges Association, the Associated Colleges of the Midwest, the Union for Experimenting Colleges and Universities, the League for Innovation in the Community College. Another is the annual conventions of state, regional, and national associations. A third is through informal cooperation such as the following:

> *The forty-five community college presidents of southern California are getting together each summer at Lake Arrowhead for three days of unstructured conversation, with the Community College Leadership Program of the University of California at Los Angeles making arrangements and doing the bookkeeping.*

> *The provosts of seven research-oriented institutions (California Institute of Technology, Carnegie-Mellon, Case Western Reserve, Johns Hopkins, MIT, Rochester, and Washington University) have begun conferring on a monthly basis.*

> *The Ford Foundation has given $15,000 during each of the past two years to permit semi-annual two-day conferences of the deans and a second representative of the undergraduate colleges of eight major universities: Chicago, Columbia, Cornell, Harvard, MIT, Princeton, Stanford, and Yale.*

> *Seventy-six representatives from sixteen cluster colleges met in November 1969 for an informal conference at Justin Morrill College at Michigan State and found the sessions so useful they planned periodic reunions—the first of which attracted three hundred participants to the University of Michigan in the fall of 1970.*

> *Representatives of academic consortia have been conferring twice yearly at a consortium seminar*

during the annual meetings of the American Council on Education and the American Association for Higher Education.

Not only are state officials concerned with higher education getting together for national meetings (such as the thirty-nine executive officers of statewide boards of higher education, the directors of facilities commissions, state scholarship programs and loan programs, and directors of continuing education) but the Education Commission of the States has now organized a Council of Higher Education Agencies where the officers of these five separate associations can meet.

Even professors of higher education are beginning to organize. Over six hundred faculty members currently teach courses in higher education, and after an ill-fated attempt by the Carnegie Corporation and W. H. Cowley over a decade ago to develop interchange among them, some of them have been meeting annually at the American Association for Junior Colleges and American Association of Higher Education conferences and are on the verge of developing an association.

Foundations have occasionally assisted in such meetings. The Rockefeller Foundation has helped underwrite Victor Butterfield's Special Committee on Liberal Studies, which has held regional meetings with selected scholars to stimulate humanistic education. And Ford, Rockefeller, and the Edgar Stern Foundations have supported the work of Martin Meyerson and Stephen Graubard's Assembly on University Goals and Governance, which has operated through several councils and seminar groups made up of representatives of various institutions. Most periodic meetings, however, can be financed from institutional resources and left to the spontaneous initiative of the individuals involved. There is usually some way or other to get together.

37

COOPERATIVE RESEARCH

Beyond these visits and meetings, a number of administrators want access to comparative data on practices and policies of institutions that are similar to theirs and on topics ranging from techniques of running registration efficiently to the budgets for computer operations. They cannot use national statistics as fruitfully as those from their peer institutions. The dean of a community college offered an example of the problems involved. He wanted comparable facts from the thirty-six other community colleges in the state of New York regarding their policy of paying faculty members to coach sports—a practice not permitted with state funds but followed nonetheless by some of the institutions. No one in the state had this information and so he and his institutional research assistant spent a total of sixty-two hours getting the facts from twenty-three of the colleges and then sharing the conclusions with them.

Some cases of data-sharing already exist, such as these involving student data:

> *Thirteen small colleges have cooperated for the past five years in a study of student development at their campuses—a project funded by the National Institute of Mental Health and directed by Arthur Chickering at Goddard College.*

> *Four hundred colleges and universities participate in the cooperative research program of the American Council on Education, obtaining data on their freshmen's attitudes, interests, and activities in comparison with those from groups of similar institutions among the four hundred.*

> *Six universities active in the development of cluster colleges are sharing data about their students*

from using ready-made survey questionnaires—the two University of California campuses at San Diego and Santa Cruz, Florida University, the University of Kansas, the University of Michigan, and the University of the Pacific.

Similar projects are under way within consortia and state and regional associations. Additional sharing of data can easily be organized informally among interested institutions. In 1968, for example, at the University of South Carolina, Laurence Flaum, the assistant to the president for special projects, put together and began circulating a monthly newsletter on *Innovation and Innovative Programs* that described educational experiments at the university and elsewhere. By mid-1970, when Flaum moved to direct institutional studies at the Medical University of South Carolina in Charleston, he was mailing over 1,300 copies throughout the university and to over one hundred cooperating institutions as far away as Australia.

CONCLUSIONS

The United States possesses an unsystematic system of higher education. Its colleges, universities, and other post-secondary educational institutions form an interdependent system in which developments at one institution or in one sector have repercussions elsewhere—as when the emergence of community colleges adversely affects neighboring private colleges and proprietary technical schools. But communication within the system is not systemic, for higher education still retains some of the characteristics of a cottage industry. Its institutions, although not as isolated from each other as are the even more provincial social institutions of the neighborhood school and the neighborhood church, remain unnecessarily separated and thus inefficient.

Information Services for Academic Administration

The essence of a cottage industry lies in its production of identical piece-work by scattered and parochial units of manufacture, among them families and farms. Too many colleges retain this spirit. Their presidents and some of their faculty may be able to get away once a year to the outside world, but basically they operate in a local league with local contacts and local limitations. Among all institutions of higher education, they are most in need of wider communication. Lacking it, they waste their limited resources on inappropriate equipment—the wrong computers, dysfunctional television studios, expensive science supplies. And in curriculum planning they reinvent the wheel.

Breaking this vicious cycle requires cosmopolitan contacts: personal acquaintance with additional sources of information and example. In 1966, the Interuniversity Communications Council proposed a spectacular nationwide information network that would help reduce this isolation. Dubbed EDUNET, this multimillion dollar transmission system would involve leased-line circuits for computer and closed-circuit television relays, facsimile reproduction, and voice communication for sharing teaching, research, and administrative data.[1] Sections of such a system are already in small-scale operation and ultimately something like the comprehensive EDUNET system will evolve. But improved communication among institutions does not require a million dollars a year as would the proposed leased electronic circuits of EDUNET. It could entail, as Dennis Binning suggests, some well-placed telephone credit cards. And it would involve funding for two clearinghouse and data-bank projects.

First, the Association for Institutional Research should

[1] See G. W. Brown, J. G. Miller, and T. A. Keenan, *EDUNET: Report of the Summer Study on Information Networks Conducted by the Interuniversity Communications Council (EDUCOM)* (New York: Wiley, 1967), pp. 359–360.

become a major facilitator of interinstitutional communication. Founded five years ago by leaders in institutional research, the Association today has a membership of some eight hundred institutional research specialists and has the potential for becoming a significant organization. So far, however, it has concentrated its limited resources on an annual workshop conference and it is only now beginning to attract widespread interest among the new breed of computer-oriented analysts and planners that universities are hiring to supplement their institutional research staffs. Foundation investment in providing full-time staff for the Association could lead to its becoming an association for institutional research, analysis, and planning, and it could then become the clearinghouse for information about current studies and the stimulus for cooperative inter-institutional research.

For Information

Wilber Tincher, Secretary
Association for Institutional Research
Director of Educational Services
Auburn University
Auburn, Alabama 36830
(205) 826–4000

Second, beyond unilateral and ad hoc cooperative projects such as those the Association for Institutional Research could facilitate, a central agency is needed as a data bank to permit institutions to get comparative facts from groups of selected colleges without corresponding with the separate institutions involved. A college that wants to compare its performance or characteristics with similar institutions should not have to collect for itself any existing standardized data. Ultimately, therefore, the National Center for Educational Statistics of the United States Office of Education should be staffed to be able to respond to requests for data on selected institutions from its annual Higher Education General Information Surveys. If this proves impossible (as seems all too likely from past experience), the American Council on Education Office of Research, with its own computer-tape copies of Office of Education data, is the next logical facility. A vitalized Association for Institutional Research might be a third possibility. Such a center could not only provide tailor-made comparative data at cost for institutions, it could become a storehouse of institutional study reports that were contributed by individual colleges and universities, with the capability of reproducing copies for distribution to other interested institutions.

Except for foundation support for these limited projects, the expansion of communication among institutions can and should be accomplished largely by institutions themselves.

5

Institutes and
Workshops

This year witnessed an addendum to the Peter Principle that "in a hierarchy every employee tends to rise to his level of incompetence."[1] Now Paul Armer, the director of the Computation Center at Stanford, has stated the Paul

[1] L. J. Peter and R. Hull, *The Peter Principle* (New York: Morrow, 1969), p. 25.

Principle: "Individuals often become, over time, uneducated and therefore incompetent at a level at which they once performed quite adequately."[2] The primary means of avoiding the fate of the Paul Principle in most professions is by continuing education through conferences and workshops. Higher education, interestingly enough, has not been as systematic as other professions in the development of continuing education for its administrators. Instead it has relied on the annual meetings of associations, where association business is ratified in ill-attended sessions.

Association meetings are of course useful: they permit communication, relaxation, escape, diversion, junketing, and hopefully some help. But except for the chance to meet friends and colleagues in hotel rooms and lobbies, they are by and large talkathons. They offer administrators the opportunity to sit on hardbacked hotel chairs and listen to speeches rather than to have to read them; but an administrator need not journey to Washington or Chicago to hear notables: he can hear them as well on a tape recorder at home with his shoes off.

"The primary value of going to conventions is discussing mutual problems with known friends," says one university provost. "The convention problem is finding one's own friends." But administrators attend them, if only in desperation and only if they can safely leave the campus, even though conventions do not meet many of their needs. As David Riesman says:

[2] P. Armer, "The Individual: His Privacy, Self-Image and Obsolescence," in *The Management of Information and Knowledge: A Compilation of Papers Prepared for the Eleventh Meeting of the Panel on Science and Technology*. Committee on Science and Astronautics, United States House of Representatives (Washington, D.C.: United States Government Printing Office, 1970), p. 79.

Institutes and Workshops

The things they need to know on the job are of such detail and intricacy that the two- or three-day meetings, for example, of the American Council on Education cannot do much for them. They cannot learn, in such a forum, how to handle police and the different types of police, and what sorts of force can be counted on from local and state patrolmen, the National Guard, student guerrillas, and community vigilantes. Indeed, people do not enter graduate work in history or in physics, or enter the seminary, in order one day to have to be expert in the use of controlled force.[3]

For the foreseeable future at least, the majority of academic administrators will not have graduate training in academic adminstration besides their work in history or physics, and thus the need for better in-service education than that of the annual association convention remains critical.

THE NEED

Only two out of seventy-two administrators who responded to a survey by Bill D. Feltner at the University of Georgia saw no value in either administrative workshops, seminars, or internships;[4] and among the suggestions we received from administrators for this study, 14 per cent called for more institutes and conferences. Sidney Tickton, of the Academy for Educational Development, identified one reason for this large a percentage when he commented to us, "You can't help the president at his desk. You've got to take him

[3] D. Riesman, "Vicissitudes in the Career of the College President," speech given at the dedication of the O. Meredith Wilson Library, University of Minnesota, May 13, 1969.

[4] B. D. Feltner, *College Administrators: Present and Anticipated Needs in Selected Colleges* (Athens, Georgia: Institute of Higher Education, University of Georgia, 1969).

away from his office and relieve him of responsibility from time to time. Executives are badly in need of some respite, as well as knowledge."

Among the respondents to our survey, some advocated broad-scale administrative development institutes, such as those of the American Council on Education's Institute for College and University Administrators, while others wanted brief, quickly-called workshops on specialized issues of immediate concern. Some suggested wider participation by business managers, comptrollers, registrars, admissions officers, and others. And several asked that programs such as those of the Institute for College and University Administrators not be limited to novices, but instead be opened to experienced executives who want additional education.

The existing programs do not meet the demand. The three most recent dean's institutes of the American Council received a total of 549 applications for a maximum of 120 places; the Institute for the Study of Change at Claremont could admit only twenty out of seventy-five applicants; and the recently-formed commerical seminars have succeeded because the nonprofit organizations had not met the need.

Cost is a major limitation. The nonprofit associations claim they require subsidy in order to run adequate sessions since charging the full cost to the registrants prohibits the poverty-stricken college from participating. As an example, the intensive sessions for presidents and deans run by the Institute for College and University Administrators are widely applauded, for one reason because they are limited in size to permit frank and informal interchange between the members and a large number of case leaders and speakers. But during their fifteen years of operation each participant has been subsidized over $700 through the $1 million of outside support that the institute has received from Carnegie and other foundations. Now being forced to move toward full-costing of its programs, the institute has reluctantly upped its deans' charges to $400 and its presidents' fees to $675, realizing that a third of the applicants to the president's institute in June 1970 required financial assistance in order to attend.

It may never be possible to develop an equitable pattern of financing continuing education in academic administration that would balance costs to the individual participant, his institution, and society at large in terms of the benefits each derives from the training. But colleges and universities should continue to budget greater support for in-service training of their staffs, above and beyond attendance at conventions, as they have done with sabbaticals for faculty. Aid from the federal government for continuing education through the Education Professions Development Act is highly desirable as a supplement, but only as that: its grants justifiably are limited to partial support and are inadequate stipends by themselves for anyone who has not taken vows of poverty.

Funding, in short, remains a problem; but simply pouring more funds into the present system of training would be uneconomic. Other problems exist that unless met would drain away the benefits of support. As we see them, these five improvements are most pressing:

Coordination

Planning for future institutes deserves coordination. Better distribution of programs among positions (ranging from department chairmen to trustees), among institutions, and among geographic regions seems mandatory, and is a logical responsibility of the American Council on Education. Conferences that have deserved repetition have been one-shot ventures; publicity has been erratic; sequential programs have been a rarity. Higher education can learn lessons here from hospital administration. The field of hospital administration, as part of its development into a profession during the past thirty years, has organized a coordinated program of continuing education for its members that puts academic administration to shame. The reason, of course, is that hospital administration has become a professional career. No longer is it simply the province of physicians who happen to be administratively inclined, unlike higher education where academic administrators are often still viewed as side-tracked scholars.

A four-level series of in-service education programs is now available for hospital administrators. First, the several conferences and seminars run by the professional association of the field (the American College of Hospital Administrators) aim at developing general administrative skills. They include an annual four-day Congress on Administration held in Chicago, at which some twenty seminars are each repeated two times so that participants can attend three; a series of forty three-day seminars on executive skills held during the year at locations throughout the United States and Canada; and an annual tour of health services in a foreign country such as Sweden, England, or Australia. Second, the thirty-five university schools of hospital administration operate postgraduate programs, aimed originally at the administrators of small hospitals who had not graduated from the two-year master's degree program of the schools. Besides short-term seminars for middle-management staff, several of the schools have developed year-long study programs consisting of two weeks of summer courses, eleven months of home study and monthly meetings with a preceptor, and a final university course of one or two weeks. Third, regional hospital assemblies as in New England, the middle-Atlantic states, and the tristate area of Indiana, Illinois, and Wisconsin, permit staff members from the seven thousand hospitals of the nation to meet annually. And fourth, state and local hospital associations hold

48

one-day and two-day forums and seminars which are open to department heads as well as central administrators.

As a result, the field is covered—so much so that Clement Clay, the director of the program in hospital administration at Columbia, says that the only remaining need is for enough time for administrators to attend all of the available programs.

In the legal profession the Practicing Law Institute conducts many weekend seminars at regional centers around the country on short notice whenever important changes in the law occur, to help practicing lawyers keep up to date. Within the federal service, the Federal Executive Institute is holding eight-week training programs five times a year at Charlottesville, Virginia, for high-level civil service employees. Within business and industry, of the five hundred largest corporations in the nation, at least three hundred have management training programs for their administrators, using either internal staff or university schools of business. But higher education itself lacks comparable training.

Team Orientation

Most institutes for academic administrators are individually-oriented rather than team-oriented. Only the workshops of the Danforth Foundation and the University of Georgia, those of the American Management Association and the National Training Laboratories, and a few seminars by Higher Education Executive Associates have sought to educate teams—either teams of administrators on the one hand, or representatives from administration, faculty, students, and governing board on the other. In essence, higher education has emphasized homogeneous representation from heterogeneous institutions. It needs in addition programs aimed at heterogeneous representation from homogeneous institutions, with attendance by varied members of similar institutions. Moreover, rather than simply mixing together participants from academic institutions, these academics could gain perspective from meeting with administrators of other types of organization—health agencies, government departments, the schools, and business. Says one college president who attended a conference of this type by the American Management Association, "Rather than talking shop with other college presidents, I listened to men from a variety of fields and we got down to real organizational problems."

Cumulation

Few programs are cumulative: they neither build sequentially on previous programs nor aim at continued self-education in the future, in terms of learning how to continue learning. Most do not aim even at helping their participants disseminate their own learning to their colleagues back home. They are not, in short, really *continuing* education but only segmental stop-gaps. In this connection, a university president advocates a monthly seminar for perhaps a dozen administrators, with two-day meetings on such issues as open admissions, black studies, investments, or faculty unionization, and with staff assistance to plan sessions, arrange for speakers, and assemble data and readings.

Involvement

Academic in nature, most institutes still consist of lectures to the participants. They could on the one hand employ more active learning (for example, problem solving, simulation, and case studies) or at the other extreme they could be far less structured than they now are to permit more individual conversation. Listening to an off-the-record talk by an experienced executive about his work can be as educational as either a lecture or a case study; but few institutes have been designed to stimulate frank information communication. One experienced official laments that "one trouble in trying to get new presidents together is that they don't tell the truth to each other." And at a recent meeting of deans from eight major universities, one participant had to plead, "Since we're among friends, it would be nice if we all made a statement about what we're actually doing as opposed to what we've said in public. I'd be interested in hearing what's going on at other institutions—not what is being considered, but what is actually happening."

Evaluation

Few conferences and institutes are intensively evaluated and altered as a result. Among the few: the summer workshops on liberal arts education of the Danforth Foundation, where Laura Bornholdt visits each of the participant colleges within two years to see what effects the workshop has had, and the Administrator Development Program of the University of Georgia, where Bill D. Feltner does the same thing within one year. At the moment, top priority should be assigned to a training conference for conference directors themselves, where they could consider better techniques of evaluation and teaching and also plan more coordinated programs of in-service education for the future. Encouragingly enough, if some university were to sponsor such a training institute, federal funds under the Education Professions Development Act would likely be available to help support it.

Information Services for Academic Administration

PRESENT PROGRAMS

Existing programs range from the weekend airport-motel workshop to the nine-month postdoctoral university fellowship; from the completely unstructured bull-session to the routinized training program; and from the frankly commercial, such as the two-day seminars on Grantsmanship for Higher Education that the ubiquitous Governmental Management Institute runs every few weeks at $185, to the slyly promotional, such as the all-expense-paid Executive Seminars that the American College Testing Program has held for college presidents in Fort Lauderdale and for state directors of higher education in Colorado Springs.

Major Programs

Below is a list of the major programs now in operation, beginning with those that are open to any institution and ending with those that are restricted in terms of membership or available through invitation.

THE INSTITUTE FOR COLLEGE AND UNIVERSITY ADMINISTRATORS

This institute of the American Council on Education runs the most extensive and elaborate series of meetings of any educational association. Theoretically open to any institution, publicity about the institutes is mailed only to ACE member institutions and to individuals who specifically request announcements. The 1969–1970 sessions included these seven: The annual President's Institute for forty chief administrators with not more than five years' experience in the position, with a coordinate program of education for the presidents'

52

wives and with tuition of $825 for six days and room and board of about $30 a day. Four five-day Dean's Institutes in Chicago, Chapel Hill, Denver, and St. Louis, each for forty participants. The Denver and St. Louis sessions received $9,000 apiece in funds from the Education Professions Development Act, and charged $25 registration fees; tuition at the other two was $475. A five-day institute for chief business officers in New Orleans, cosponsored by the National Association of College and University Business Officers on a $12,000 budget with $250 tuition. An experimental two-day invitational institute for trustee-and-president teams from some twenty institutions, at $100 per person with the difference coming from $8,000 of residual Carnegie funds.

Prior to its move to the ACE in 1965, the institute operated for a decade as a private trust under Robert Merry's direction at the Harvard Business School on the basis of $924,000 from the Carnegie Corporation. Since then it has received $68,000 from Danforth and smaller grants from Hazen and Sears-Roebuck, but it was recently precariously existing on residuals and $30,000 of the general operating funds of ACE until the Mellon Foundation rescued it with $75,000 for the next three years. Caught between a format of the most costly sessions in the field and belt-tightening particularly among the most impecunious institutions, the institute is moving toward full-costing its programs, and is using its foundation grants to subsidize attendance from impoverished colleges and to update its basic repertoire of case studies.

Information Services for Academic Administration

	Evan Collins, Director; Charles F.
For	*Fisher, Program Director*
Information	*Institute for College and*
	University Administrators
	American Council on Education
	One Dupont Circle
	Washington, D.C. 20036
	(202) 833–4781

THE INSTITUTE FOR EDUCATIONAL MANAGEMENT

In 1969, this institute organized out of the Harvard Business School with a grant of $280,000 from the Sloan Foundation to run a six-week summer program in 1970 and again in 1971 for sixty middle-management college administrators and a few executives from business. Aimed at developing a comprehensive rather than a specialized view of the management of educational institutions, the institute is bringing together presidents, deans, business managers, and financial development officers to analyze close to a hundred case studies and listen to a dozen guest lecturers on four main topics: managing the educational institution, information systems for planning and control, management of funds, and human behavior and organizational problems. In 1970, six Harvard Business School faculty members, a former HBS faculty member, and President Paul Sharp of Drake made up the teaching staff. The Sloan funds are paying the $1,600 tuition for the academic representatives, but their institutions are expected to pay the $950 room and board.

Institutes and Workshops

For
Information

*Winfield Knopf and
John W. Teele, Codirectors
Institute for Educational
Management
Holyoke Center–625
1350 Massachusetts Avenue
Cambridge, Massachusetts 02138
(617) 547–1472*

THE AMERICAN MANAGEMENT ASSOCIATION CENTER FOR PLANNING AND DEVELOPMENT

Recently this center began two academic administration programs at its Hamilton, New York, facilities: First, a five-day management course for college and university presidents, at $700 including room and board. And second, an adaptation for higher education of the Team Process in Corporate Planning of the American Management Association, in which a team of up to fifteen decision-makers of an institution comes to Hamilton for a week of institutional self-analysis, followed by a month during which the AMA staff puts together data about the institution as a result of the self-analysis, and then another week-long meeting to study the conclusions and agree on future actions. So far the center has run this program for five colleges at a charge of $10,000 each plus $2,500 for team room and board.

For
Information

*Franklyn S. Barry, Director
The Center for Planning and
Development
American Management
Association, Inc.
Box 88
Hamilton, New York 13346
(315) 824–2000*

55

Information Services for Academic Administration

NTL has been expanding its original sensitivity training human relations sessions into organizational development, including higher education. It runs Presidents' Conferences on Human Behavior for seven days periodically in Palm Beach, Nassau, or Carlsbad, California, and in 1970 scheduled a three-part twelve-day Higher Education Laboratory Program at Plymouth, New Hampshire, which included: (1) A program for teams from colleges and universities, with some time devoted to each team's own particular project but much time spent on the process of team building and team analysis, (2) a basic human relations laboratory, typical of the ordinary sessions of NTL, but specifically for student leaders, and (3) an advanced laboratory for faculty members and graduate students, aimed at developing their general competence in informal or formal group leadership. Costs for the sessions at Plymouth ran $325 for faculty members and $225 for students, plus $160 room and board. For 1971, NTL plans similar programs in New England and in Cedar City, Utah.

For *Information*	*Richard D. Albertson, Director* *Center for Educational Studies* *National Training Laboratories* *Institute for Applied Behavioral* *Science* *1201 Sixteenth Street, N.W.* *Washington, D.C. 20036* *(202) 223–9400*

THE PLANNING AND MANAGEMENT SYSTEMS PROGRAM

This project of the Western Interstate Commission for Higher Education is running three-day seminars on a first-

Institutes and Workshops

come, first-served basis in Boulder, Colorado, to institution and agency representatives from throughout the country to explain not the abstract philosophy of planning and management systems but the nuts and bolts of Management Information Systems tools which WICHE has been developing with federal funds for national implementation: its program classification structure, its resource requirements prediction model, and the like.

For Information	*Robert Huff, Training Coordinator* *Planning and Management Systems* *Program* *Western Interstate Commission* *for Higher Education* *Post Office Drawer P* *Boulder, Colorado 80302* *(303) 449–3333*

University Programs

University programs in higher education have emphasized preservice training to the detriment of continuing education, but these inservice programs are in operation:

KELLOGG CENTERS

Eleven centers of the Kellogg program for leadership in community colleges are charged with providing inservice education. For example, the UCLA center has held an invitational workshop during each of the past three summers: the first for presidents, the second for deans of instruction, and the most recent for new trustees; with one in 1971 planned for presidents again. The eleven Kellogg centers are at Berkeley, UCLA, University of Colorado, University of

57

Florida, Florida State, University of Michigan, Michigan State, Teachers College, University of Texas, University of Washington, and Wayne State.

UNIVERSITY OF GEORGIA

The University of Georgia runs a program for recently appointed second-echelon college administrators under Title III of the Higher Education Act. On the average, twelve administrators a year attend from both two-year and four-year institutions. The program involves a one-week seminar, a week-long visit to other campuses, a second one-week seminar, a consultative visit from Bill D. Feltner during the academic year, and finally two two-day follow-up conferences by the end of the academic year. In 1970, Feltner has also developed a series of seminars for administrative teams from ten colleges in the southeast under a $30,000 Education Professions Development Act grant.

UNIVERSITY OF MICHIGAN

The Center for the Study of Higher Education of the University of Michigan holds an annual five-day institute on college and university administration, utilizing current and former Michigan professors as the faculty. In addition, the university runs the only post-doctoral program of which we know. Three or four faculty members or administrators a year participate as visiting scholars in weekly seminars, administrative meetings, group travel, and an internship at the university. Until 1968, Carnegie funds provided fellowships for the visiting scholars; but now they must support themselves and consequently half of them can stay only a semester.

Institutes and Workshops

Besides its series of specialized conferences, The Berkeley Center for Research and Development in Higher Education continues to cohost an annual summer conference on a topic of general concern with the Western Interstate Commission for Higher Education.

COLUMBIA UNIVERSITY

The Graduate School of Business of Columbia University plans an Arden House meeting for sixty college presidents in collaboration with the Academy for Educational Development.

EDUCATION PROFESSIONS DEVELOPMENT ACT PROGRAMS

The biggest boom in university programs is stemming from Title E of the Education Professions Development Act of 1967, which provided $6.9 million in 1969 and $10 million in 1970 to universities for short-term programs, institutes, and graduate fellowships for educators. Most of the resulting programs and fellowships are for specialists in academic subjects; some are for student personnel administrators; and only a few have been for central administrative personnel of colleges and universities. For example, out of the $5 million available in 1970–1971 to underwrite ninety-three short-term training programs and institutes, only $554,000 was allocated for fourteen programs in higher educational administration. And of the other $5 million to support graduate fellowships for educators at seventy-seven universities, only six of these universities have EPDA fellowships for higher education administrators—for a total of fifty-one fellowships out of all 902.

Information Services for Academic Administration

	Higher Education Personnel
	Training Programs 1970–1971,
For	*OE–58028–71*
Information	*Publications Distribution Branch*
	United States Office of Education
	Washington, D.C. 20202

Commercial Programs

Two commercial firms are conducting short training programs for college and university administrators:

SYSTEMS RESEARCH GROUP

SRG is running two-day and three-day planning and budgeting seminars once a month in Toronto, based on Richard Judy and Jack Levine's development of Comprehensive Analytical Methods for Planning in University Systems (CAMPUS). In two days at $200 they demonstrate their approach to institutional planning, which embraces management information, resource simulation models (the heart of the CAMPUS program), and planning, programming, and budgeting systems, with third- and fourth-day technical sessions available at $100 each, plus room and board.

Institutes and Workshops

Systems Research Group
252 Bloor Street West
Toronto 5, Ontario, Canada
(416) 964–8411

For
Information

Systems Research Group
370 Lexington Avenue
New York, New York 10017
(212) 686–5378

Educational Systems Research
Group
1601 Connecticut Avenue, N.W.
Washington, D.C. 20036

HIGHER EDUCATION EXECUTIVE ASSOCIATES

The consulting and conference enterprise formed by Thomas Emmet in 1967, and acquired in 1969 by McGraw-Hill, offers seminars on a variety of hot specialized topics: two-day workshops with four or five experts giving papers and being available for individual assistance, at fees of $175 for the first representative, $120 for the second, and $90 for students, all plus room. The most ingenious of the past sessions of HEEA was a seminar traveling through California in 1970 to visit a number of cluster colleges. Among those planned for 1970–1971: labor negotiations, academic advising, conflict resolution, campus discipline and justice, and a tour of Canadian universities to examine unicameral governance.

For
Information

Higher Education Executive
Associates
230 W. Monroe
Chicago, Illinois 60606
(312) 368–6500

Information Services for Academic Administration

Chief Executive Programs

Two programs designed for chief executives of various types of organization may be of interest to academic administrators:

THE PRESIDENTS ASSOCIATION, INC.

This branch of the American Management Association offers a comprehensive inservice training program for managers. Initially the chief administrative officer attends a five-day Management Course for Presidents at $650 plus room and board. Then he can send a team of his immediate officers, such as vice presidents, to a three-day Top Management Briefing at $424. Next the president can attend a special two-day session on The Chief Executive and the Board of Directors, or his key board members may attend The Corporate Board Member—His Roles and Responsibilities. Finally participants in the Top Management Briefings can send members of their own staffs to three-day Middle Management Briefings so that they will also know how to work as a team.

For Information	*Allen Mathis* *American Management Association, Inc.* *135 West 50th Street* *New York, New York 10019* *(212) 586–8100*

THE ASPEN INSTITUTE FOR HUMANISTIC STUDIES

This institute has run its Aspen Executive Program since 1950: a two-week great-books-and-volleyball session limited to eighteen participants and their auditor wives. The members are expected to read the assigned books, ranging from Pericles to Martin Luther King, Jr., in advance, and be prepared to discuss their significance during the morning seminar meetings, with recreation scheduled in the afternoon and lectures and concerts in the evenings. Cost: $1,200, including room and board, plus $350 extra for wives.

	William E. Stevenson, President
	Aspen Institute for Humanistic
For	*Studies*
Information	*Post Office Box 219*
	Aspen, Colorado 81611
	(303) 925-7010

Restricted Conferences and Workshops

Turning to the conferences and workshops that are restricted to particular institutions either because of association sponsorship or because of invitation, most of the national associations of higher education institutions hold conferences for their constituents in addition to their annual meetings. For example:

THE AMERICAN ASSOCIATION OF STATE COLLEGES
AND UNIVERSITIES

AASCU runs a biennial summer council for its presidents and their families—eighty-six of whom attended the 1969 session in Estes Park and discussed state-wide planning, campus governance, minority groups, student activism, and collective bargaining.

Information Services for Academic Administration

THE AMERICAN ASSOCIATION OF COLLEGES FOR
TEACHER EDUCATION

AACTE holds its own biennial School for Executives in the off-years of the AASCU, with the fifteenth held in 1970 at the University of Virginia. A fourth of the one hundred or more participants are presidents; the rest are education deans and faculty members. Outside speakers, panel discussions, and informal conversation comprise the program, with family activities planned by the National Association of Wives of Presidents and Deans of Member Institutions of AACTE.

THE AMERICAN ASSOCIATION OF JUNIOR COLLEGES

Through its Facilities Information Service, the AAJC has sponsored an air-borne tour by trustees, presidents, and architects of planned two-year colleges to visit outstanding examples of college design and construction.

THE ASSOCIATION OF AMERICAN COLLEGES

AAC once organized the Pugwash conferences, held on philanthropist Cyrus Eaton's Nova Scotia estate and devoted to the discussion of philosophical issues by scholars and administrators. Now it holds a special session prior to its annual convention each January for any new presidents of member institutions, both to get acquainted and to discuss problems that they have suggested in advance, such as handling the press and getting along with trustees.

Institutes and Workshops

CASC held four programs in 1970: two institutes on management training for the presidents of its eighty-three colleges; its fourteenth annual summer workshop at which the academic dean and two faculty members from each of thirty colleges worked on an institutional project; and a five-day institute covered by an EPDA grant to permit a trustee, the president, and the director of development from up to eighty colleges to concentrate on development plans, with follow-up consultation to each institution provided during the academic year by experienced development officers from other institutions.

THE COUNCIL OF GRADUATE SCHOOLS

CGS held its third summer workshop for graduate deans in 1970 at Brainard, Minnesota. One hundred and twenty deans came to Lake Arrowhead the previous summer, with their universities paying travel and sustenance and the council budgeting its own funds for honoraria and proceedings.

THE NATIONAL ASSOCIATION OF COLLEGE AND
UNIVERSITY BUSINESS OFFICERS

A busy association, NACUBO cooperated on the business officer's institute last year with the Institute for College and University Administrators of the ACE, ran a senior accounting officer's workshop in St. Louis, and held five elementary workshops on planning, budgeting, and accounting for small colleges in Dallas, Los Angeles, Columbus, Philadelphia, and Atlanta. Two hundred and sixty attended the five sessions, priced at $60 for the first participant and $40 for the second, with the content built on Daniel Robinson's *A College Operating Manual, Part Two: Planning, Budgeting, and Accounting* from Peat, Marwick and Mitchell, which NACUBO has published.

THE AMERICAN COLLEGE PUBLIC RELATIONS ASSOCIATION

In 1970 ACPRA held four national conferences, a summer academy, training institutes, workshops, and its annual regional district conferences.

THE SOCIETY FOR COLLEGE AND UNIVERSITY PLANNING

The society held its fifth annual conference in 1970 at the University of Massachusetts, and focused on studies of recent facilities planning there and elsewhere in the state.

THE WESTERN INTERSTATE COMMISSION
FOR HIGHER EDUCATION PROGRAM

The largest program ever organized to help educate department chairmen to their responsibilities was coordinated during 1968–1970 by the Western Interstate Commission for Higher Education under a $100 thousand grant from the Danforth Foundation. Aimed at trying a variety of inservice training programs for eventual adoption by more institutions, the WICHE effort met some resistance from central administrators of universities who did not want it indoctrinating their novice department chairmen, division heads, and deans. But WICHE succeeded in these activities: a regional conference at Lake Arrowhead; area-wide conferences for administrators and department chairmen at Cedar City, Utah, and Helena, Montana; periodic meetings of chairmen of sociology departments in the Colorado-Wyoming region and of chairmen of English departments elsewhere; and state-wide conferences in Arizona, California, New Mexico, Oregon, and Washington. Among its singular accomplishments were the first meeting in history of the department chairmen of Utah State University with its academic vice-president and its budget officer to discuss issues of financial management, and the first meeting of department chairmen at New Mexico to discuss their own responsibilities as chairmen.

DANFORTH FOUNDATION PROGRAMS

Finally, two programs operated directly by the Danforth Foundation deserve description and commendation. Its Workshop on Liberal Arts Education, organized in 1957 and currently directed by Laura Bornholdt, brings four-man teams (including a student at institutions where students share in policy formation) from between twenty-five and thirty colleges to Colorado Springs each summer for a two and one-half week workshop. Mornings are devoted to seminars, led recently by such notables as Clark Byse, Joseph Katz, Morris Keeton, Lewis Mayhew, Walter Metzger, and James Redfield, and afternoons are reserved for group work on a project to be implemented back on the home campus. Danforth invites institutions to participate and pays all of the nontravel expenses involved (including $300 fellowships to those faculty members not on twelve-month appointments) out of an annual appropriation of approximately $75 thousand.

Danforth's Institute for College Development was a twelve-month invitational program run by David Zimmerman for seven Appalachian region colleges and seven Great Plains colleges to help them survive. The institute began with an eight-day conference in 1969 for central administrators and two faculty members from each college on institutional problems and prospects, continued with a meeting of presidents and trustee and faculty representatives to discuss regionalism and regional service as a possible goal for the colleges, permitted each institution to use up to $2,000 for consultation or other development work, and ended in 1970 with a ten-day workshop on a particular project for implementation at each college. The institute cost $125,000 in all, and Danforth is evaluating its results before deciding about repeating it in the future.

CONCLUSIONS

Every profession as it matures moves from apprenticeship training of its new members to formal instruction both for them and for the continued education of its present practitioners. Professional schools of hospital administration, medicine, business, and public administration have organized in-service training programs for the practicing specialists in their fields, and university departments of higher education have begun to offer some in-service training for current administrators. But the bulk of continuing education for academic administration continues to be offered by the several professional associations themselves. Much more is needed, but much more than simple expansion is required. Continuing education for college and university management should be more widely distributed, better coordinated, more cumulative, more intensive, and better evaluated.

Financial aid for workshops and institutes under the Education Professions Development Act has been of great benefit and deserves continuation. But the academic community should not rely on the Office of Education to organize a comprehensive and coordinated program of continuing education for higher education administration. This is the responsibility of the academic community itself—and in particular of the major coordinating body within higher education: the American Council on Education. Planning such a program will involve other associations, university centers, foundations, and the Office of Education, but leadership in planning is imperative. Little excuse exists for academic administration to lag so dismally behind the comparable field of hospital administration in assuring its own professional development.

6

Publications

$\mathbb{D}$uring a recent eight-day period William Kelly tallied for us his incoming correspondence as president of Mary Baldwin College. The results: three questionnaires; six books; ten professional journals and two *Saturday Reviews;* twelve pamphlets, brochures, or reports; sixteen announcements or advertisements; twenty-one newsletters and weekly newspapers; and some seventy letters, part of which were mass mailings. Kelly says that he has wondered about hiring a vice-president in charge of mail to see that it gets routed and circulated correctly.

Publications

Concerning routing and circulation, another president of our acquaintance calculated for us how he disposes of incoming publications: 40 per cent forwarded to the staff after he skims them; 10 per cent routed directly to individuals without skimming; 10 per cent sent on directly to the library; and 20 per cent destroyed—part of them unopened. But this still leaves 20 per cent that he sets aside on the window sill behind his desk to read but does not get to—including the *Educational Record, Change,* and *College and University Business.*

The frustration stemming from these piles of unread publications seems nearly endemic among academic administrators. Of all channels of information for them, print is the most oversaturated. Part of this problem stems from the pressures of administration and possibly from the very temperament of administrators. "Presidents are audile types," suggests James Perkins in discussing the problem. "They're ear-minded. They're not verbile—they're not readers. That's why telephones are far more important to presidents than any publication." An additional part of the frustration stems from the nature of periodicals themselves. They arrive in the mail on the publisher's schedule and with only the publisher's best guess of his readers' interests and needs. They cannot be directed to immediate action.

But a major problem is simply that most educational literature is useless as information. It is prolix, redundant, trivial. "Why human problems and human results must be so drearily discussed is a perplexing mystery," wrote Benjamin Lieberman in 1960 in a study for the Fund for the Advancement of Education of the problem of educational literature. He observed, "The educational journals, professional organizations, and their communication methods (conventions, papers, and so on) are conservative or deadly dull (which effectively enforces the status quo). . . . Most education

71

journals are so deep in old ruts that they may be inextricable."[1] And as a result, the fund decided to avoid professional literature and to underwrite instead the educational supplement of the *Saturday Review*.

In 1963, Ronald A. Wolk, at Johns Hopkins University, took eight months off to study the publications problem specifically of higher education for the Carnegie Corporation and Editorial Projects for Education. Among his conclusions were these comments:

> *Both because they are so numerous and because they are often not well-edited, the specialized publications generally appear to fail to reach their audiences effectively. . . . There is much duplication in the publications of the education associations, a number of which have overlapping membership lists. The holder of multiple memberships must wade through essentially the same material over and over, to find the few unique items of information. . . . Professional leaders, their desks cluttered with printed materials, need a means of finding relevant information quickly and systematically. No truly effective "digest" publication now exists. No newspaper-fast reporting of the entire field of higher education is now available. . . . Members of the horse-racing fraternity, fans of baseball, investors in stocks receive complete daily statistics within hours, . . . while persons in education must wait for months and sometimes years for the data they need.*[2]

Conditions have improved since Wolk's report, if only because of the resulting actions taken by director Corbin

[1] J. B. Lieberman, "Seven Strategies," a memorandum for the Fund for the Advancement of Education, 1960.

[2] R. A. Wolk, *Disseminating Information About Higher Education* (Baltimore: Editorial Projects for Education, 1963), pp. 3, 4, 32.

Publications

Gwaltney at Editorial Projects for Education and by the Carnegie Corporation. Gwaltney had been responsible for transforming the Johns Hopkins alumni magazine into an outstandingly intelligent journal, and had organized EPE to publish interpretive articles on issues in higher education for insertion into college alumni magazines. On the basis of Wolk's study, Carnegie gave EPE $68,500 to begin its *15-Minute Report to College and University Trustees,* and when Gwaltney found out that college presidents themselves were reading the *15-Minute Report* for news, he got $220,000 more from Carnegie to launch *The Chronicle of Higher Education*—now the most informative publication in the field of higher education at large.

Gwaltney and William A. Miller, Jr., the managing editor, have made the *Chronicle* into the *Wall Street Journal* of higher education, combining fast news and feature stories with pick-ups of data that used to get published slowly or distributed narrowly, like the AAUP's salary ratings and the tabulations of state appropriations for higher education, compiled by M. M. Chambers, at Illinois State University. More administrators tell us they read it than any other educational publication. But despite the improvement stemming from the *Chronicle,* the conclusions that Lieberman and Wolk reached about educational publications still hold true for most other periodicals. They still are loosely edited and unsystematically planned. Few have undertaken readership surveys. Some, subsidized by their association's membership fees, appear to be primarily vehicles for demonstrating that the association does in fact exist. And their numbers increase. One recent tally listed ninety-six periodicals in higher education, not to count the occasional reports and one-time studies, monographs, and books. Within the junior college field alone, for instance, the American Association of Junior Colleges publishes ten separate newsletters besides its monthly *Junior College Journal;* and

Information Services for Academic Administration

Arthur Cohen, the director of the ERIC Clearinghouse for Junior College Information, says that the additional JC literature now comes to several books a year, a number of state education department publications, a hundred dissertations, and hundreds of indigenous reports "ranging from 'This is the way we do it at our school' to listings of data gathered for no apparent reason."[3] The reader still finds himself confronted with too much reading.

THE NEED

According to the college administrators we have questioned, their first and most common unmet need regarding educational literature is for metainformation materials—that is, for reference guides to the literature, and in particular for abstracts of what is important through some type of alerting or skimming service. Note the similarity in these comments from among the 15 per cent of our respondents who mentioned this need:

> *An alphabetized system of abstracting—an index, in other words, which separates the wheat from the chaff and gets a busy administrator to substantive information without having to wade through all the baloney.*

> *A monthly index or directory . . . with annual compilations of all topics appearing in the various sources of data.*

> *A simplified bibliography that could keep us abreast of new professional developments and procedures, . . . together with instructions as to how to obtain materials.*

[3] A. M. Cohen, "Who is Talking to Whom," *Junior College Research Review,* 1969, *3* (8), 7.

Publications

Dissemination of research on management. We don't want to go through Dissertation Abstracts to find it.

A kind of information bulletin specializing in abstracts of court decisions on campus problems—or of ideas and developments about job responsibilities— or the structure of administration.

Some resources in this direction already exist, such as Brent Breedin's *Education Abstracts* at the American College Public Relations Association and the various syntheses of Lewis Mayhew, professor of higher education at Stanford, for the American Association for Higher Education, and they are welcomed. But they do not yet meet the need, both because the topics of concern to administrators are so varied and because the literature on them is so extensive, with many of the most important ideas appearing outside the education journals in such sources as *Psychology Today, Daedalus,* and *The New York Review of Books.*

One way to meet this need would be to expand the metainformation function of existing publications such as *Education Abstracts, The Chronicle of Higher Education,* and the American Council on Education newsletter, *Higher Education and National Affairs.* Another could be through a new abstracting publication aimed directly at higher education as neither *Education Recaps, Current Contents,* nor ERIC's *Research in Education* is. And a third could be the creation of temporary newsletters on hot issues that would emphasize metainformation. The Carnegie Commission on the Future of Higher Education, directed by Clark Kerr, has discussed the need for such short-term publications in the areas of equal opportunity and of black studies, and Kerr recommends their creation. So far, however, the commission has not publicly called for them because it has not been able to agree who should publish them.

The second major request beyond abstracts is for authoritative syntheses of information on particular problems. More than simple compilations of available resources, these would be in-depth interpretive analyses. Note the suggestions here:

> *Intelligently edited descriptions of new curricular approaches and changes in governance forms.*

> *A Journal of Academic Administration, . . . a clearinghouse to collect and diffuse information on problems, with each issue devoted to one topic.*

> *A kind of analog to the Kiplinger Letter for higher education—oriented toward the future, concentrating on likely issues to which institutions must probably work out some appropriate mode of address.*

> *Analysts who would attempt to give us some insight not only as to trends but the degree of success of a number of innovations.*

> *A publication wherein an entire issue is devoted to a particular problem in higher education, that is, management information systems, registration, student behavior, faculty governance, and so on.*

Here again the need is partially met, and may lie as much in not knowing where to find these analyses as in their nonexistence. The ERIC clearinghouses are beginning to publish integrative syntheses of research findings and of significant educational practices. Gwaltney and Miller are expanding their interpetive articles in the *Chronicle,* and the American Council on Education is assisting through its series of *Special Reports* on topical issues. There is still hope that *Change* magazine may meet this need, too, although so far it has not. Dreamed up by Samuel Baskin of Antioch and other representatives of the Union for Experimenting Colleges and

Universities as a trading post to alert educators to innovations elsewhere, it has taken a different tack under George Bohnam's editorial direction and Esso's $455,000. Its former editor, Peter Schrag, contended that *Change* was not in business to help administrators with recipes and reports about present programs but instead to develop a concern among laymen, legislators, and educators for novel and untried options to the present collegiate system. Thus *Change* has aimed at analyzing the basic philosophical issues confronting higher education and examining the underlying epistemology of the academy. Whether it will do more than this in the future under new editors is so far unclear.

A few of the administrators we have questioned recommend the creation of a new general magazine about higher education, comparable to *Trans-action* or *Psychology Today,* that would be informative for laymen as well as for professors. (In 1961, Gwaltney at Editorial Projects for Education developed a prototype of such a magazine called *Renaissance* that could still be resurrected, and John Caffrey, former director of the Commission on Academic Affairs at ACE, wanted the American Council to start one titled *Campus USA.*) But the overwhelming consensus among administrators points not to the development of more periodicals but to major reforms in the existing ones, and in particular to increasing their locator or metainformation function and the scope and penetration of their analyses. In short, better data, not more.

PRESENT PUBLICATIONS

The Chronicle of Higher Education, followed closely by the American Council's *Higher Education and National Affairs,* lead by far the list of publications that our respondents

Information Services for Academic Administration

told us they read. Next in order, although some distance from these two, are the monthly and bimonthly newsletters and magazines. Trailing behind are the traditional academic journals such as the *Journal of Higher Education* and *Liberal Education.* Some presidents may find time to read them, and they are read by staff members and professors of higher education. But they get brief mention in comparison to the more frequent news publications. For informing academic administrators, the era of the academic quarterly appears over.

Many significant articles for administrators appear outside the educational press, but here are some thirty publications of note within the field of higher education. (A more extensive list can be found in *An Annotated Guide to Periodical Literature—Higher Education,* by T. J. Diener and D. L. Trower, published in 1969 and available for $.50 from the Institute of Higher Education, University of Georgia, Athens, Georgia 30602.)

News

THE CHRONICLE OF HIGHER EDUCATION

Now a weekly except during the summer months, the *Chronicle* covers more news in more depth in less space than any other educational publication. Skillfully edited and attractively printed, it aims to become even more substantive with more in-depth analyses. Editors Gwaltney and Miller are satisfied that it has enough credibility by itself apart from the Washington higher education establishment that they have moved its offices there from Baltimore. Circulation, nearly twenty thousand with hopes of forty thousand when its current $300 thousand grant from Ford expires in 1974. Subscriptions, $15.

Publications

For Information

The Chronicle of Higher Education
1717 Massachusetts Avenue, N.W.
Washington, D.C. 20036
(202) 667-3344

HIGHER EDUCATION AND NATIONAL AFFAIRS

This main newsletter of the ACE would more aptly be titled "Higher Education and *Federal* Affairs," since it primarily reports federal activities related to colleges and universities, with some news about higher education above and beyond ACE actions. Fast, but factually, factually factual, as edited by Frank Skinner, ACE's Information Officer. Circulation, twenty thousand distributed on a quota system to ACE member institutions and sent to individual subscribers at $25 a year for approximately forty issues.

For Information

Higher Education and National Affairs
American Council on Education
Suite 800
One Dupont Circle
Washington, D.C. 20036
(202) 833-4700

Abstracts and Indexes

EDUCATION ABSTRACTS

This is the best-written summary available of higher education topics appearing in the educational and lay newspapers and journals. Succinct and wide-ranging, as written by Brent Breedin. Circulation, 5,800 a month, with 3,600 going to ACPRA representatives at member institutions and the rest to college presidents who have indicated they would like to receive it. Subscriptions, $8.50.

For *Information*	*Education Abstracts* *American College Public* *Relations Association* *Suite 600* *One Dupont Circle* *Washington, D.C. 20036* *(202) 293–6360*

EDUCATION RECAPS

In this monthly newsletter, Ann Smith at ETS condenses news about all levels of education from other publications, including the *Chronicle,* and press releases from institutions, foundations, research and development centers, government agencies, and educational laboratories. Broadening for anyone who does not mind skimming through elementary and secondary news, too. Begun as an internal newssheet to keep the ETS staff informed about educational developments, it is now mailed to three thousand individuals at $3. For ten or more copies the price is $1.50 each.

For *Information*	*Education Recaps* *Educational Testing Service* *Princeton, New Jersey 08540* *(609) 921–9000*

RESEARCH IN EDUCATION

This journal of abstracts is published by ERIC and contains about fifty abstracts a month from each of the ERIC

Publications

clearinghouses on fugitive literature such as institutional reports or occasional speeches—copies of which can then be ordered through the ERIC Document Reproduction Service. Subscriptions, $25.

	Research in Education
For	*United States Government*
Information	*Printing Office*
	Washington, D.C. 20402

CURRENT INDEX TO JOURNALS IN EDUCATION

This publication is a monthly counterpart to *Research in Education,* but indexing articles appearing in 534 journals rather than any unpublished documents, and containing only title, author, and subject listings instead of abstracts. Subscription, $34 a year for non-cumulative issues; $64 with semiannual and annual cumulations.

	Current Index to Journals in
	Education
For	*CCM Corporation*
Information	*909 Third Avenue*
	New York, New York 10022
	(212) 935-2000

COLLEGE STUDENT PERSONNEL ABSTRACTS

Emily Starr edits this quarterly summary of articles, reports, and convention papers concerning student personnel at the higher education level. Circulation, 1,700. Subscriptions, $20.

	College Student Personnel
For	*Abstracts*
Information	*College Student Personnel*
	Institute
	165 East Tenth Street
	Claremont, California 91711
	(714) 624–3595

CURRENT CONTENTS

This new series of weekly bulletins reproduces the contents pages of every conceivable journal in each of seven fields, the two of potential interest to academic administrators being *Current Contents—Education* and *Current Contents— Behavioral, Social and Management Sciences*. Each series covers about seven hundred publications, and so it is too extensive in scope to be widely useful for the practicing administrator. Subscriptions, $67.50 per series.

	Current Contents
For	*Institute for Scientific Information*
Information	*325 Chestnut Street*
	Philadelphia, Pennsylvania 19106
	(215) 923–3300

Journals

CHANGE

Change is the one hopeful sign on the journal horizon, with large aims but with difficulties in meeting everyone's diverse expectations and in solving transiency among its editors. It aims to be written in English in order to attract readers outside of education, and while it is not turning out

82

Publications

to be the trading post of information about innovation that some had hoped, it is at least a signpost pointing in interesting directions. Circulation of eleven thousand with hopes of breaking even at thirty thousand. Subscriptions at $8.50 for six bimonthly issues.

For Information

> *Change*
> *59 East 54th Street*
> *New York, New York 10022*
> *(212) 753–8302*

JUNIOR COLLEGE JOURNAL

JCJ is the snappiest of all the educational journals, showing evidence that its editor, Roger Yarrington, heeds its art director. The major publication of the American Association of Junior Colleges, its circulation of nearly fifty thousand is exceeded in higher education only by the *AAUP Bulletin*. Nine issues a year at $4.50.

For Information

> *Junior College Journal*
> *American Association of*
> *Junior Colleges*
> *Suite 410*
> *One Dupont Circle*
> *Washington, D.C. 20036*
> *(202) 293–7050*

EDUCATIONAL RECORD

The most substantial of any of the journals, the *Record* is substantially predictable as the rotund voice of the academic establishment since 1920. Circulation, ten thousand copies distributed to member institutions and associations of the ACE, plus two thousand subscriptions at $10 for four quarterly issues.

For *Information*	*Educational Record* *American Council on Education* *Suite 800* *One Dupont Circle* *Washington, D.C. 20036* *(202) 833–4700*

COLLEGE AND UNIVERSITY JOURNAL

Aimed by Brent Breedin of ACPRA at college advancement officers (PR and development men) in order to "enable them to perform their responsibilities wisely and well," *College and University Journal* contains some articles of general interest by a variety of luminaries. Circulation, 4,300. Subscriptions at $9.50 for six bimonthly issues.

For *Information*	*College and University Journal* *American College Public* *Relations Association* *Suite 600* *One Dupont Circle* *Washington, D.C. 20036* *(202) 293–6360*

LIBERAL EDUCATION

This quarterly, devoted to undergraduate education, contains tweedy, genteel essays, filled with "shoulds" and "oughts" about the curriculum, along with some squibs from college press releases at the back in "Among the Colleges." Circulation, 4,500, including copies to the 890 member institutions of AAC. Subscriptions at $5.

Publications

For
Information

Liberal Education
Association of American Colleges
1818 R Street, N.W.
Washington, D.C. 20009
(209) 265–3137

THE JOURNAL OF HIGHER EDUCATION

The only journal of higher education run by a university press, it is most precarious, with nothing but a developing affiliation with the American Association for Higher Education to sustain it. Variable in depth and coverage, and indistinguishable from the other quarterlies. Circulation, climbing over 3,500. Subscriptions, nine issues a year at $8 except $6 for AAHE members and $10 for libraries.

For
Information

The Journal of Higher Education
Ohio State University Press
2070 Neil Avenue
Columbus, Ohio 43210
(614) 293–6930

COLLEGE AND UNIVERSITY BUSINESS

McGraw-Hill publishes this trade journal for higher education and distributes it free to administrative officers, on a quota basis, of all colleges and universities over two hundred in enrollment. Under Dennis Binning's editing, it is becoming editorially substantial on educational issues and is losing its fixtures-and-food-service stereotype. Thirty thousand free subscriptions through Controlled Circulation, *College and University Business,* Post Office Box 607, Hightstown, New Jersey 08520. Individual subscriptions at $15 for twelve monthly issues.

Information Services for Academic Administration

	College and University Business
For	*230 W. Monroe*
Information	*Chicago, Illinois 60606*
	(312) 368–6500

COLLEGE MANAGEMENT

A journal acquired two years ago by Crowell-Collier-Macmillan, it squeaks along on little advertising but some substantive articles and a number of "how we do it here" descriptions. Free circulation of twenty thousand to administrators of all colleges and universities over 2,500 and a few innovative colleges under that size. Other subscriptions at $15 for twelve monthly issues.

	College Management
	CCM Professional Magazines, Inc.
For	*22 West Putnam Avenue*
Information	*Greenwich, Connecticut 06832*
	(203) 869–8585

AMERICAN SCHOOL AND UNIVERSITY

This journal bills itself as "The Buildings Magazine," and it is that and nothing more. Mostly advertisements. Acquired, along with its companion International College and University Conference and Exhibition Program, from Buttenheim by North American. Total circulation, 41,600, with some 11,000 going free to college and university presidents, business managers, and directors of buildings and grounds. Otherwise $8.

Publications

For
Information

American School and University
North American Publishing
Company
134 North 13th Street
Philadelphia, Pennsylvania 19107
(215) 564–5170

AAUP BULLETIN

The annual salary report of the *Bulletin* is "probably the most assiduously read document in American higher education," in the words of one university vice-president, but the *Bulletin* contains as well hypnotically troubling committee reports on academic freedom and tenure cases, AAUP policy statements, and an infrequent but hilarious academic satire. Circulation, 96,000. Subscriptions, $4.50 for four quarterly issues plus the occasional newsletter of AAUP.

For
Information

AAUP Bulletin
American Association of
University Professors
Suite 500
One Dupont Circle
Washington, D.C. 20036
(202) 466–8050

SATURDAY REVIEW

The *Review* runs a twenty-four page education supplement every month, with articles and news about education at all levels. Subsidized originally by the Fund for the Advancement of Education, it is now underwritten by the Kettering Foundation. Circulation, six hundred thousand. Subscriptions, $10 for fifty-two weekly issues.

Information Services for Academic Administration

For
Information

Saturday Review
380 Madison Avenue
New York, New York 10017
(212) 983–5555

Newsletters

CIRCULAR LETTER

Of all the association newsletters, the best by far is this publication of the National Association of State Universities and Land-Grant Colleges. It has been limited to less than two thousand copies and distributed only to state colleges and universities and land-grant institutions.

HIGHER EDUCATION IN THE STATES

This is a new informative monthly publication from the Education Commission of the States, supplementing and supplanting in news for higher education both ECS's general monthly newsletter, *ECS Bulletin,* and its bimonthly journal, *Compact.* Edited by Nancy Berve, it contains much factual material on state policies. Circulation, five thousand. Free. (ECS is also publishing occasional papers and reports, such as R. F. Carbone's *Resident or Nonresident? Tuition Classification in Higher Education in the States,* Report Number 18, for $1.)

Publications

For Information

Higher Education in the States
Education Commission of the
States
822 Lincoln Tower
1860 Lincoln Street
Denver, Colorado 80203
(303) 255-3631

RESEARCH REPORTER

The *Reporter* contains synopses, observations, and conclusions from recent research on American higher education, primarily that conducted by the staff of the Center for Research and Development in Higher Education at Berkeley. Circulation, 7,500. Free.

For Information

Research Reporter
Center for Research and
Development in Higher Education
University of California, Berkeley
Berkeley, California 94720
(415) 642-5040

EPE 15-MINUTE REPORT FOR COLLEGE AND UNIVERSITY TRUSTEES

This semimonthly newsletter interprets developments in higher education selectively and succinctly. Read twice as frequently by trustees as any other periodical in higher education, according to Rodney Hartnett's survey of five thousand trustees three years ago. Circulation, four thousand. Subscriptions, $12.

Information Services for Academic Administration

For *Information*	*EPE 15-Minute Report* *Editorial Projects for Education* *1717 Massachusetts Avenue, N.W.* *Washington, D.C. 20036* *(202) 667–3344*

AGB REPORTS AND AGB NOTES

Both of these are J. L. Zwingle's publications for trustees at the Association of Governing Boards. The quarterly *Reports* contain speeches and reprints of articles in some length. *Notes* began last year on a monthly basis with quick news of interest. Circulation: the six thousand trustees who are members of the 315 boards belonging to the Association. No subscriptions: only institutional memberships at $150 to $875.

For *Information*	*AGB Reports or AGB Notes* *Association of Governing Boards* *of Universities and Colleges* *Suite 720* *One Dupont Circle* *Washington, D.C. 20036* *(202) 296–8400*

COLLEGE PRESS SERVICE

An assemblage of news stories related to colleges, college students, and social concerns, this newsletter is mailed daily during the academic year and less often during the summer primarily to campus newspapers that pay from $100 to $450 a year for reprint rights. Less costly to nonpublishing subscribers. Edited this year by Nicholas DeMartino at the United States Student Press Association (the association of four hundred student newspapers).

Publications

*For
Information*

College Press Service
1779 Church Street, N.W.
Washington, D.C. 20036
(202) 387–7575

THE ACQUAINTER

A newsletter about and for academic consortia, *The Acquainter* is edited by Lewis D. Patterson and published by the consortium of the Kansas City region. Free, to 1,700 subscribers.

*For
Information*

The Acquainter
Kansas City Regional Council
for Higher Education
Suite 320
4901 Main Street
Kansas City, Missouri 64112
(816) 561–6693

EDCENTRIC

This more-or-less monthly newsletter about educational developments and reforms is published by the National Student Association. Free to impecunious individuals, but with a $5 or so donation requested from affluents and institutions.

*For
Information*

Edcentric
Center for Educational Reform
National Student Association
2115 S Street, N.W.
Washington, D.C. 20008
(202) 387–5100

91

Information Services for Academic Administration

INTERCULTURAL EDUCATION

This new monthly newsletter has an imaginative and distinctive format: ten or so loose-leaf sheets, each devoted to a different topic within intercultural and international education; all within a double-fold cover containing a general story. One sheet may be an excerpt from a speech or article; another, news of new developments in foreign study or area studies. Circulation, ten thousand. Free.

For Information	*Intercultural Education* *International Council for* *Educational Development* *522 Fifth Avenue* *New York, New York 10036* *(212) 867–9450*

REPORT ON QUESTIONNAIRES

This monthly newsletter describes all questionnaires known to be circulating within higher education, as reported to its editor, Sybil Weldon, at the ACE by fifty campus representatives who serve as watch posts. Even if the *Report* has not reduced the number of questionnaires, it has publicized their existence and the means of obtaining data resulting from them. Subscriptions, free to ACE member institutions and associations; otherwise $5.

For Information	*Report on Questionnaires* *American Council on Education* *Suite 800* *One Dupont Circle* *Washington, D.C. 20036* *(202) 833–4700*

Publications

A newsletter of information on state appropriations and legislation for higher education, it is assembled by M. M. Chambers and has been published gratis first by the University of Michigan beginning in 1958, then by Indiana, and now by Illinois State. Circulation, under one thousand, to particularly interested individuals. Free.

	M. M. Chambers
	Department of Educational
For	*Administration*
Information	*Illinois State University*
	Normal, Illinois 61761
	(309) 438–7655

COLLEGE AND UNIVERSITY BULLETIN

This newsletter of the AAHE periodically contains a section entitled "So They Say About Higher Education," a summary of selected articles assembled by Lewis Mayhew. Circulation, over seven thousand. (Mayhew also summarized *The Literature of Higher Education During 1969* in a $2 booklet available from the association.)

	College and University Bulletin
	American Association for
	Higher Education
For	*Suite 780*
Information	*One Dupont Circle*
	Washington, D.C. 20036
	(202) 293–6440

File Materials

The next two publications provide reference data on federal programs: (For a "Listing of Operating Federal Assistance Programs," see the House of Representatives document 91–177 by that title, available for $4.50 from the United States Government Printing Office, Washington, D.C. 20402.)

COLLEGE AND UNIVERSITY REPORTS

This biweekly service of Commerce Clearing House for higher education is comparable to its reports in other professional fields. Each mailing is in two parts: a summary report of new federal developments related to higher education, and then loose-leaf pages either replacing or adding to existing cumulative volumes about federal legislation, regulations, and rulings. Sponsored originally by nineteen major universities and the American Council on Education, it is designed for the broad needs of research-oriented universities. Subscriptions, $500 a year or $455 for each of two years.

For *Information*	*College and University Reports* *420 Lexington Avenue* *New York, New York 10017* *(212) 689–5233*

GUIDE TO FEDERAL ASSISTANCE

Appleton-Century-Croft produces this blue filing box on federal programs. $375 for the first year, including the box, and $225 for succeeding years, with each month bringing a packet updating the materials.

Publications

For
Information

Guide to Federal Assistance
New Century, College Division
440 Park Avenue South
New York, New York 10016
(212) 689–5700, extension 249

A FACT BOOK ON HIGHER EDUCATION

The *Fact Book* contains statistics compiled from a variety of federal surveys and other sources about higher education, displayed historically and graphically to show trends. A useful but under-used book from the American Council on Education. Allan Ostar of the State Colleges Association says, "Not a day went by when I ran the Joint Office of Institutional Research when I didn't get a call from a president wanting some information—and it was right in the *Fact Book*." Circulation, 1,400 free copies to ACE members and one thousand to nonmembers at $35.

For
Information

Fact Book on Higher Education
American Council on Education
Suite 800, One Dupont Circle
Washington, D.C. 20036
(212) 833–4700

NACUBO PROFESSIONAL FILE

This file was begun as an occasional supplement in depth to the NACUBO newsletter, *The College and University Business Officer*. The first three issues consisted of a good speech on labor-management relations in higher education by Lee Belcher, of the University of Missouri, a critique of the Ford Foundation recommendations regarding total return on investments, and another of the revised *College and Univer-*

sity Business Administration. Circulated to member institutions of NACUBO.

For Information	*NACUBO Professional File* *National Association of College and University Business Officers* *Suite 510* *One Dupont Circle* *Washington, D.C. 20036* *(202) 296–2346*

Book Publishers

Among book publishers, McGraw-Hill and Jossey-Bass are publishing the bulk of volumes relevant to the administration of higher education. McGraw-Hill is printing the reports stemming from the Carnegie Commission on the Future of Higher Education and has released the two-volume *Handbook of College and University Administration,* edited by Asa S. Knowles and priced at $70.

For Information	*McGraw-Hill Book Company* *330 West 42nd Street* *New York, New York 10036* *(212) 971–3333*

In San Francisco, Jossey-Bass is continuing to broaden its research-based series of books on higher education, and has inaugurated a companion series of shorter "state-of-the-art" books on particular college and university problems. In the planning stage is a series in teacher education, a loose-leaf case book on the law and higher education, a monthly subscription service of brief loose-leaf reports on topics of concern to administrators, and a research journal for the field entitled *New Directions in Higher Education.*

	Jossey-Bass, Inc., Publishers
For	*615 Montgomery Street*
Information	*San Francisco, California 94111*
	(415) 433–1740

Internal Circulation of Publications

Even if colleges do not appoint vice-presidents-in-charge-of-mail to handle the distribution of these and other publications, they can employ other means to circulate them. Beyond the typical routing cycle, some institutions Xerox the tables of contents of incoming publications as they arrive and circulate copies to key officers. Some prepare listings of major news stories about higher education from the daily press or make Xerox copies of the stories for circulation.

The most extensive program of disseminating news about the literature of higher education to administrators has been developed by Wayne State University. With aid from the Office of Education, it set up in 1964 a computerized abstracting service called a "Selective Dissemination of Information" system. The system is operated by the Administrative Reference Center of the Office for Institutional Research at Wayne State. Twice a month the center sends to administrators short abstracts (such as the following example) that its staff has prepared on recently received books, articles, reports, and legislative acts. The uniqueness of the system lies in the fact that each administrator has specified the subjects in advance in which he is particularly interested, and only the abstracts containing references to these subjects are printed out by Wayne State's computer onto IBM cards and sent to

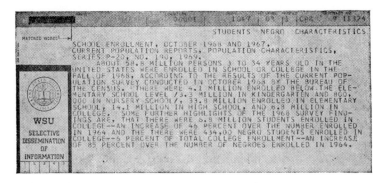

him. If he then wants to read the complete document itself, he marks the card and returns it to the center.

Currently two staff members of the center are scanning about 120 publications a month, including journals, monographs, and the *New York Times,* and abstracting from them roughly one hundred items each month. Ninety administrators, both at Wayne State and at ten other Michigan colleges and universities, are receiving the abstracts; and discussions are under way about the possibility of extending this service at cost to other institutions.

CONCLUSIONS

The system at Wayne State offers the most sophisticated operational prototype that we know of for trying to match mechanically the available literature in higher education to the interests of individual administrators. Eventually this type of service should be available to officers of any institution as part of a metainformation system for college and university administration. But it would be uneconomical for other universities themselves to duplicate this service, and for Wayne State and the ERIC clearinghouses concerned with higher education to duplicate their abstracting activities. Between Wayne State, ERIC, and other interested agencies, an abstracting service could be developed on a subscription basis that could supply its readers with abstracts in areas of particular interest to them.

Two other more immediate steps can meet the needs of administrators in the meantime. First, the existing system of abstracts can be strengthened. Between Lewis Mayhew for the American Association for Higher Education, Brent Breedin at *Education Abstracts,* Emily Starr at the College Student Personnel Institute, and the staffs of the ERIC Clearinghouses, enough expertise exists to plan a series of top-flight abstracting publications for higher education, more comprehensive and less redundant than the present system. This improvement should come about through alterations in present publications, with the creation of new periodicals such as temporary topical newsletters and bibliographies as a reluctant alternative.

Second, more agencies should undertake authoritative syntheses of information on topics of current concern. Naturally all publishers hope to print only authoritative reports: comprehensive, synoptic, useful documents. No one publisher could be expected to corner this market, although several of them are interested in trying to provide educators with the information they need—among them, Corbin Gwaltney at *The Chronicle of Higher Education,* Dennis Binning at *College and University Business,* Allen Jossey-Bass at Jossey-Bass, Inc., Publishers, and the directors of some of the ERIC clearinghouses. Their efforts in this direction should find ready endorsement as well as the gratitude of administrators and specialists in higher education, besieged as they are with printed fluff and published filler.

7

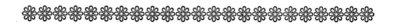

Consulting Services

Every administrator seems to have his own favorite horror story about consultants. Among them:

> *The little college that did not realize it had been had until its president noticed that its consultant had given him the same recommendations that he had made to an industrial corporation—having neglected*

to change his references in his report from "shop fore-men" to "department chairmen."

The eastern university that paid a consulting firm ten thousand dollars to find it a director of development who lasted one year, leaving the university in the market for his successor.

The sixty thousand dollar fee from one major management consulting firm for recommending the replacement of three confused staff members with nine confused staff members.

The private university that poured three hundred thousand dollars into an accountant consulting firm in hopes of getting an administrative data system, all to no avail; and whose vice-president finally admitted, "We didn't know what we wanted, and they didn't know how to do it."

The consulting business is naturally vulnerable to such disparagement since clients may feel demeaned by their need for help and may slight in hindsight the aid of the helper. But outside counsel is necessary periodically in most organizations, and even Harvard has recently had McKinsey and Company examine its administrative structure. An outsider can bring additional perspective to the analysis of problems, lend credence to new ideas, pour oil on internal feuds, and point out unnoticed inefficiencies—such as closing down the computer at five o'clock.

Of all the information services available to college and university administrators, consultation is most frequently requested. Eighteen per cent of the administrators we queried for this report mentioned it as a need—more than any of the other needs they reported. And of all types of information service, consultation can be the most directly helpful by bringing expertise to bear on particular problems at particular times. But for this very reason it is the most expensive form of information service—and the most open to shysters.

THE NEED

A few universities tend to rely too often on outside consultants rather than in-house expertise, hiring high-priced firms and being left in the lurch by them rather than developing competence among their own staff. Some others have obtained continuing counsel by retaining a permanent consultant for periodic visits—as Rochester Institute of Technology has done with Ralph Tyler. The majority, however, seem to hunt for counsel too infrequently, too late, and for the wrong reasons—to mop up the results of crises rather than help prevent them; to answer questions rather than raise them; to find more money rather than to help make its use more effective.

Administrators report that they can use advice on topics ranging from the development of specialized expertise in computer installations to the location of competent and available consultants. Two needs dominate, however: better access to a broader range of talent for small scale assistance; and better information about, and surveillance of, the consulting field itself.

Access to Small Scale Assistance

Institutions could benefit greatly from timely, short-term counsel. One eastern college, for example, asked Heald Hobson to estimate the cost of a feasibility study on coeducation for the college. The reply: four months' time and $27,000 —and so the college trustees decided to go coeducational without a study. A few days of help from some expert source, however, should have been available to this institution and to others like it. George Arnstein reports from his study of the response of higher education to recent social problems, "A very large number of college administrators . . . admit freely that they simply do not know what to do. They face a new ballgame with new rules, or worse yet, with no rules at all. They need help. But, and this is crucial, *there is no place where they can get help.*"[1]

Arnstein advocates a Campus Consulting Council to make technical assistance available to administrators by telephone or by quick visit. Some aid could be highly specialized on legal issues, minority problems, security measures, and other concerns, but some could be simply hand holding, whereby an elder statesman could commiserate with a frantic administrator or help field ideas within an administrative council. The Administrative Consultant Service that the Association of American Colleges has run since the late 1950s has demonstrated the utility of hand holding, but AAC itself recognizes the still unmet need for highly-skilled specialized counsel.

Some observers of college administration advocate a small full-time staff of specialists for such a campus consulting council; but a better long-term solution lies in locating and developing consulting ability among ever-widening numbers of people. The most radical suggestion in this direction has been made by Morris Keeton, head of Antioch, Columbia. He has pilot tested a plan for home growing consulting teams consisting of administrative, faculty, student, and possibly trustee members from an institution who would visit a second campus that was having internal difficulties, talking with their counterparts during the day to learn different perceptions of the problems and then comparing notes during the evening to try to

[1] G. Arnstein, "What Is Higher Education Now Doing, for Better or for Worse?" paper presented at the Twenty-fourth National Conference on Higher Education, Chicago, Illinois, March 3, 1969.

piece their findings together. After witnessing this experience, members of the host institution would be able to participate in a second visit to another campus. In this way, each institution would teach another; and the pool of potential advisors could be expanded indefinitely.

We favor such means of developing more informal and cooperative consulting rather than relying exclusively on professionals. The professional management consulting and development firms play a necessary role in advisement; but the full-time consultant, whether in a firm or moonlighting from a campus, is subject to the temptation of hoarding his knowledge for profit and sharing his expertise only for a fee. This proprietary attitude toward knowledge is antithetical to the professional responsibility of the educator, who is expected to share his knowledge broadly for the public good; and colleges and universities should aim to broaden the sources of available counsel beyond full-time consultants.

The best informed individuals are already over-committed. One outstanding college president receives an average of fifteen calls a week from colleagues asking for his help; the advice of one foundation officer to Yale about its obligations regarding minority problems was so skillful that he has had to decline additional requests to repeat his work at other universities; an economics professor undertaking a survey of self-studies found that he had rapidly become the authority on the field and was himself being called on for counsel, without time to spare. Moreover, the knowledgeable individual fears the possibility of going stale by over-commitments. Thus a broader pool of expertise is needed.

Locating Qualified Counsel

Closely related to the problem of finding short-term counsel is that of knowing where to find assistance. William

Consulting Services

Jellema of the Association of American Colleges has proposed a solution to this problem—the creation for higher education of a consultant clearinghouse: an agency that would not only be able to refer institutions to expertise, but also would evaluate the work of experts. He observes:

> *New agencies offering to provide expert counsel come into being much faster than their ability to perform can be evaluated by an individual college president. A fund raising firm may have been successful in the past; but what impartial, honest, yet informed comment can be obtained on its present performance? A new management consultant firm may present a handsome brochure; but how well has it performed in analyzing and recommending changes in the administrative structure of colleges? . . . What is needed is a centrally located consultant clearinghouse: a consultant advisory service that a college or university president could reach by dialing a single telephone number whenever he discovered the need for the aid of a consultant.[2]*

Jellema's clearinghouse could also help coordinate the consulting services of the scholarly associations—for example, by having the names of members of the American Psychological Association and the American Sociological Association who would be expert in evaluating an undergraduate social science curriculum.

Some administrators with the right contacts already have some of the information that Jellema proposes: they know where to get their money's worth. But, as with other areas of communication in higher education, the grapevine is parochial and restricted. It should be expanded and systematized for the benefit of all colleges and universities. A consultant clearing-

[2] W. W. Jellema, "A Consultant Clearinghouse," memorandum for the Association of American Colleges, March 13, 1970 (mimeo.).

house either at the Association of American Colleges or elsewhere, such as Jellema proposes, would help serve the needed function of metainformation—in this case, better information about the sources of expert assistance.

PRESENT SERVICES

Consulting services in higher education range from a colleague from a neighboring institution stopping by for lunch and shop-talk to a major management consulting firm redrafting the governing documents of a university as part of its continuing services to the administration and trustees. Probably three-fourths of academic consulting takes place informally with expenses and sometimes an honorarium involved; not more than a fourth would involve letters of agreement or contracts. And only a fraction of consulting has involved cooperative arrangements between one college or university and another. Such arrangements have recently been stimulated by Title III of the Higher Education Act of 1965, which has provided thirty million dollars for each of the past four years to aid "developing colleges"—those institutions "which have the desire and potential to make a substantial contribution to higher education in the nation, but for financial and other reasons are isolated from the main currents of academic life and are struggling for survival." Last year, 229 such institutions received grants to establish cooperative relationships with other, stronger institutions or with organizations and business firms. But most consulting beyond individual and informal advising is conducted by associations and corporations.

Consulting Services

Association Services

THE AMERICAN ASSOCIATION OF JUNIOR COLLEGES

More than any other association in higher education, the AAJC has tried to provide counsel for its members. It began its Facilities Information Service with support from Educational Facilities Laboratories in 1966, opened its New Institutions Program with a three-year grant of three hundred thousand dollars from Danforth in 1968, and obtained a $585,000 grant under Title III for eighty-five developing junior colleges two years ago. Each of these colleges received $7,000 for a total of seventeen man-days of consulting from a panel of some four hundred specialists in administration, curriculum, and student personnel services. In 1970, fifty-three junior colleges got $13,000 each as part of a $690,000 Title III grant to eight regional consortia of two-year institutions.

THE ASSOCIATION OF AMERICAN COLLEGES

With the initiative and support of the Lilly Endowment at approximately $35 thousand a year, the AAC conducts the Administrative Consultant Service, which has provided AAC member institutions the experience of several retired presidents for no charge except for their travel. The restricted geographic distribution of the recent consultants, however, as well as the need of AAC member institutions for more specialized advice on technical problems, has led the association to plan to point the service in new directions.

Information Services for Academic Administration

AASCU began its Consultant Service two years ago with $500 from the association treasury. Its member institutions pay the consultants' travel expenses plus $100 a day if it enrolls fewer than five thousand students and $125 if it enrolls more. John Emens runs the service out of a donated office near Ball State University at 203 North College Avenue, Muncie, Indiana 47306. In contrast to the AAC pool of only three men, Emens and his five-member advisory committee have asked over forty specialists from various institutions to participate in the thirty visits the service has so far organized.

THE COUNCIL OF GRADUATE SCHOOLS IN THE UNITED STATES

CGS has developed consultation as a major function during the past half-decade, and last year aided 125 institutions regarding plans or problems of their graduate programs. Since 1965 James M. Eshelman has administered the program as assistant to the president of the council, and in 1968 Danforth provided a three-year grant of seventy-five thousand dollars to help pay administrative costs and to subsidize the service for smaller institutions. Ordinarily a two-man team visits the institution for two days: one man from a roster obtained from the several scholarly societies, and a graduate dean from another institution. The client university pays $500 ($100 per man per day and $100 for whichever one of them writes their report) plus a $25 administrative fee to the council.

Consulting Services

CASC offers three consulting services to its members. As part of its federally-funded institute program, the participating colleges can obtain no-cost consultation from a group of outside experts. CASC retains Interagents, Inc., to provide general public relations and fund-raising counsel to member institutions, with large-scale consultation paid directly by the institutions. And Roger Voskuyl, the executive director of CASC, keeps himself available for one day of consulting per institution per year.

THE AMERICAN ASSOCIATION OF UNIVERSITY PROFESSORS

AAUP quietly works through preventive consulting to nip academic conflict in the bud rather than waiting for crisis, investigation, and possible censure. It assists nonmembers as well as members, whether or not the institution involved has an AAUP chapter or for that matter even an AAUP member. It also provides counsel to institutions by reviewing drafts of institutional policies before adoption and by intervening on request in the resolution of difficulties involving academic freedom, tenure, academic due process, professional ethics, institutional governance, student rights and freedoms, and the representation of professional and economic interests. The Washington and regional office staffs are available to visit campuses, or they may recommend other qualified persons as consultants. The staff's expenses are paid from general operating funds but those of an outside expert are paid by the institution or by the AAUP chapter involved. Problems that may have been handled summarily in the past at church-related colleges and small public institutions are now coming to the attention of the association, and its staff finds that even well-established universities continue to have problems, although of a continually more refined kind.

	Bertram H. Davis
	General Secretary
	American Association of
	University Professors
	One Dupont Circle
	Washington, D.C. 20036
	(202) 466-8050

For
Information

Matthew W. Finkin
Northeastern Regional Office
Suite 1178
11 West 42nd Street
New York, New York 10036
(212) 594-1820

Richard H. Peairs
Western Regional Office
Suite 1406
582 Market Street
San Francisco, California 94104
(415) 989-5430

THE NATIONAL CENTER FOR DISPUTE SETTLEMENT

A subsidiary of the American Arbitration Association located in Washington and headed by Willoughby Abner, a vice-president of AAA, the center had two-thirds of its staff on campuses in 1969 assisting in resolving conflicts. AAA mediators Ronald Haughton and Samuel Jackson had earlier tried to help resolve the San Francisco State College mess, and Abner himself helped resolve a dispute involving the Afro-Latin Society at Ithaca College. The center is supported by

Ford, Rockefeller and Sloan Foundation grants, but Abner hopes to form a Campus Dispute Panel of third-party mediators who would be able to spend up to five days on a problem campus at the invitation of both sides in the dispute and with expenses paid by the institution involved. The panel would also hold conferences and training courses in conflict resolution and conduct negotiations at the college and high-school level, while the National Center continued its mediating activities in civic life generally.

For Information

Willoughby Abner, Director
National Center for Dispute Settlement
Federal Bar Building West
1819 H Street, N.W.
Washington, D.C. 20006
(202) 659–5650

THE ASSOCIATION FOR COMPUTING MACHINERY

With a $70 thousand grant from the National Science Foundation, the ACM has been providing counsel to small colleges regarding the use of computers and the introduction of computer science into their curricula. William Viavant at the College of Engineering of the University of Utah is administering the program, which has involved sixteen computer experts so far in forty two-day visits to colleges, with the institutions paying only for local expenses and any travel costs above one hundred dollars. The current NSF grant will cover sixty more visits, with the possibility of renewal in the future. Viavant emphasizes that the most frequent problem of the colleges visited so far is not with deciding on computer equipment but of developing courses in and educational uses of computer science.

Information Services for Academic Administration

For
Information

William A. Viavant
ACM College Consulting Service
Post Office Box 9046
Salt Lake City, Utah 84108
(801) 322-4166

ACCREDITING ASSOCIATIONS

At the regional level, the six regional accrediting associations offer the advisement of their evaluating teams as part of their accrediting and reaccrediting function, and their small staffs spend considerable time in behind-the-scenes counseling with member institutions. The national professional accrediting organizations are offering similar services as they move beyond their earlier task of mere assessment of eligibility for approval.

Counsel on Federal Assistance

Two associations are providing consultation regarding federal assistance—the Association of American Colleges and the American Association of State Colleges and Universities.

THE ASSOCIATION OF AMERICAN COLLEGES

The AAC's Federal Relations Advisory Service, opened in 1968, is free of charge to dues-paying member institutions, and during its first year the service assisted three hundred of the nine hundred members of the association. John Talmadge at AAC headquarters directs the service as well as working on federal liaison: he answers inquiries, advises institutions about likely sources of funds for particular projects, and mails out special bulletins on deadlines and opportunities for federal funding.

Consulting Services

AASCU operates a far more ambitious and aggressive service: Office of Federal Programs. Opened in 1967 to avoid the necessity of member institutions having to retain permanent staff representatives in Washington or to hire private consultants to represent them, the office bills itself as "Your Man in Washington." Its staff of Jerold Roschwalb and five girls presently serves forty client institutions (thirty-two AASCU members and eight state universities and land-grant colleges) that yearly pay from $350 to $6,000 for assistance. The staff members help draft proposals, schedule appointments for campus representatives with federal officials, inquire about the status of applications, even make hotel reservations and provide office space and secretarial service for representatives while they are in Washington; and through a forty-two page primer for member institutions on "Gearing Up for Federal Funds," the office offers advice such as, "It behooves the applicant to be especially circumspect as he approaches the federal treasury for his share."

State Services

Only one state has so far begun to provide consulting services to the colleges and universities within its borders. The Office of Higher Education Management in the New York State Education Department offers counsel to both public and private institutions. Organized in 1961 as a result of the Heald Commission recommendations concerning higher education in the state, the office operates on a hundred thousand dollar budget—a small investment in relation to the twenty-six million dollar contribution of the state this year to private higher

113

education. Its two-man staff is in the field two to three days a week counseling with administrators at no expense to the institutions. For specialized problems it has access to some thirty consultants around the country: four of them expert in library services, two in data processing, one in buildings and grounds, another in food services, and the like. "We've had the effect of discouraging consulting firms from coming into the state," says John Haines, director of the office. "A study that a commercial firm would have to charge ten thousand to twenty thousand dollars for will cost an institution two hundred to three hundred dollars through us." Among its recent activities, the office has recommended changes in admissions practices at a private college that resulted in its recruiting nearly 150 more students last year, advised a private university on centralized versus decentralized purchasing and stores, brought an expert on food services from Illinois to analyze the problems of a seminary cafeteria, and ran up to six conferences a year: an annual meeting for trustees and presidents, another for directors of buildings and grounds, a third for administrators, and special sessions on topics such as the calendar, coeducation, and interinstitutional cooperation.

Commercial Services

Turning finally to the commercial consulting firms, 949 of them are listed by category of service (such as financial management, general management, office management, personnel management, and so on) in the *Directory of Consultant Members* of the American Management Association, available from the AMA at 153 West 50th Street, New York, New York 10020. Forty-two of the biggest management consulting firms belong to the Association of Consulting Management Engineers, located at 347 Madison Avenue, New York, New York 10017. But the biggest of the research and consulting organizations (Stanford Research Institute and Arthur D. Little, Inc.) and the biggest management consulting firm (Booze, Allen & Hamilton, Inc.) do not undertake the most educational consulting. Heading the list in the number of educational clients is Cresap, McCormick and Paget, with between twenty-five and forty projects under way for colleges and universities during each year and with half of its fifty-member staff in the Division of Health, Education, and Government specializing in education.

Among the firms specifically organized for educational consulting, the Academy for Educational Development is the largest, with a staff of fifty and some 250 occasional consultants available to it. Others, such as Heald Hobson and Associates, or Frantzreb and Pray Associates, operate with a full-time staff of up to fifteen members, and the list could include numerous smaller consortia of consultants as well as firms consisting of an individual, a letterhead, and a return address.

CONCLUSIONS

The advantages and indeed the necessity of outside counsel to educational institutions have been so amply demonstrated that colleges and universities should no longer consider consultation as an extraordinary and infrequent expense but rather as a regularly budgeted item. Just as visiting lecturers expand the educational offerings of an institution, so visiting counselors can expand the policy options of an institution. Good consultants in fact are the personification of information: they bring with them the experience of other institutions, the expertise of research literature, and the independence to raise the right questions.

Higher education at large cannot expect philanthropy to underwrite its continuing consulting needs, such as the Lilly

Endowment has provided in the past through the Association of American Colleges. Some foundation charity will continue to be required to fund crisis consulting but foundations should increasingly devote their resources to expanding the pool of available consultants and providing means for institutions to locate them—not to financing the use of consultants directly. William Jellema's proposal for a consultant clearinghouse should be implemented as the first step, both as a referral center to a greater variety of expertise and also an evaluating agency regarding this expertise.

8

Information Centers

In July 1967, the University of Texas at Austin opened a pioneering hot-line service for its students that has become a model information center: its Telephone Counseling and Referral Service at 476–7073. Manned by professionals twenty-four hours a day, 365 days a year, this service offers students information, provides immediate crisis counseling, and if necessary suggests referral to other centers

117

of help within the university. The staff (three full-time counselors and three part-timers, who work solitary eight-hour shifts) answered nearly thirteen thousand inquiries in their first year. Ninety per cent of them were simply for information, such as facts about university procedures, requirements, and activities; but the rest were for counseling—whether to drop out of school, whether to seek psychological assistance, what to do for a roommate in need of help. Only twenty-two calls out of the thousands were obviously pranks.

Since 1967, the number of calls for assistance have increased by half each year. With direct lines to the university health service and the security office in case of emergencies, the center has been able to intervene successfully in threatened suicides as well as to help solve countless routine problems. From the point of view of the university the service (budgeted at roughly fifty-five thousand dollars a year) is paying off handsomely. "It's been so successful that we now wonder why we didn't think of it before," says Tom McGee, its coordinator; and because of its success other institutions have begun to adapt the idea for their own operations.

This telephonic counseling service at Texas illustrates graphically at an institutional level the essential characteristics of an information center, which is the type of information service that is most urgently needed for higher education at large. An information center is user initiated, immediately available, problem focused, referral oriented, and authoritative and comprehensive in scope. No such service at the national level is presently available within American higher education for assistance on institutional problems. None of the existing agencies, no associations, no university centers, no government offices, not even the ERIC clearinghouses, are staffed to meet this need. And the need is obvious.

THE NEED

Most people in higher education as well as elsewhere rely on friends and acquaintances for the bulk of their information. Some have extensive contacts among knowledgeable groups, but many do not. At the same time, some knowledgeable people with authoritative expertise who would be willing to share their knowledge are unknown and unasked by the needy. Somehow the present informal networks of communication must be opened for broader and more comprehensive use.

Fifteen per cent of the administrators we surveyed pointed to this problem of locating centers of knowledge as the most urgent for improvement. Their most pressing information needs concern access to data. Do facts exist on a particular problem? Is expertise available on it? If so, where? "The plain truth of the matter is that today there is *no* source of information on general management problems in higher education, *no* place to ask for anything," says a knowledgeable Washington observer. And the recently-resigned president of a major university claims "in the United States we're at the pterodactyl level in terms of educational information—not even the Neanderthal. If you want to know how many universities have programs on Southeast Asia, or how many presidents are reaching retirement age, you can't find out."

The idea of information centers to help answer questions such as these is not new. In fields other than higher education, reference centers and clearinghouses for this purpose are already in existence, ranging from the National Library of Medicine to the American Institute of Physics and from law enforcement data centers to population statistics bureaus. Consider two examples of such information centers in other fields—one in philanthropy, the other in science—that higher education itself lacks.

Information Services for Academic Administration

With headquarters in New York, a branch office in Washington, and seven regional depositories across the country, this center is currently supplying facts about philanthropic foundations to ten thousand inquirers a year—some three thousand of them college and university administrators alone. Operating on a budget of $450,000 from twelve sponsoring foundations, the center employs twenty staff members in New York and Washington, five of whom devote full time to answering inquiries and ten of whom prepare center publications such as *The Foundation Directory*. The center is aimed primarily at public understanding of foundations, but both it and the Council on Foundations, also headquartered in New York City, can provide advice to foundations themselves on problems of their organization, staffing, programs, and reporting.

For *Information*	*The Foundation Center* *444 Madison Avenue* *New York, New York 10022* *(212) 752-1433*

THE SCIENCE INFORMATION EXCHANGE

This exchange of the Smithsonian Institution keeps computerized files on one hundred thousand federally-supported scientific research projects and employs a staff of a hundred to enter and retrieve information about them. In answer to requests about research, the staff reproduces a one-page technical summary of any appropriate project, including information about its sponsor, investigator, location, and duration, and mails the summaries to the inquirer within a few days (or in an emergency within the hour) at a cost of $40 for the first hundred summaries and $7.50 for every hundred thereafter. The exchange has been operating on a $2 million budget, but NSF wants to stop its $1.6 million contribution and so the exchange may move toward increased user fees.

For Information	*Science Information Exchange* *300 Madison National Bank* *Building* *1730 M Street, N.W.* *Washington, D.C. 20036* *(202) 381–5511*

Proposed Information Centers

So far, the higher education community has no comparable centers of information. Among the areas of information that such data centers should cover is that of consultants with particular expertise, as has been suggested by William Jellema and described in the previous chapter. Three other areas are proposed by other observers:

SOURCES AND USE OF FINANCIAL SUPPORT

Questions continually arise about federal assistance programs despite the publications and association services already available, since no central source of information within the government has data on all of them. And beyond concise information on federal programs, some administrators seek a center for information on the most effective uses of limited resources. They ask how to save money without endangering quality. What about class size? Course proliferation? Management efficiency?

CURRICULAR DEVELOPMENTS

Many administrators want to know where new educational ideas are being tried and evaluated. "Maybe the stuff is all tucked away in all of the magazines and journals that I don't read," says one of them, "but I don't know how to find out what's happening elsewhere." Examples abound: pass-fail grading; compensatory education; modular scheduling; intensive courses; work-study; developments in political science.

POTENTIAL ADMINISTRATIVE STAFF AND FACULTY

A center of information on possible candidates for employment could supplement the present informal grapevine and the consulting firms that are moving into the field of professional executive placement at a fee of 10 per cent of the salary of the first year plus expenses. No one proposes a placement center as such, but rather a matching or locator service such as that currently performed for three hundred private colleges by Mrs. Elizabeth Fisher at the Cooperative College Registry at One Dupont Circle in Washington. "We rely almost entirely on the happenstances of personal acquaintanceship, chance meetings, and random inquiry," reports one provost. "Good jobs go unfilled while good people who would fill them go undiscovered."

Centers of information on these topics are of course desirable for American higher education. They could provide authoritative and comprehensive information on specific topics on short notice for any inquirer. From our perspective, however, *the greatest need within higher education is simply for a metainformation center:* a center that knows where information exists and where data, expertise, and additional knowledge can be obtained. Such a center would not by itself be a comprehensive data bank. Instead it would be, to use Patricia Cross' imaginative phrase, a "people bank"—a center of information on knowledgeable people, whatever the issue, within higher education.

The best example of a source of metainformation in recent years for higher education has been neither an organization nor an individual but a book: Dale Heckman and Warren Bryan Martin's *Inventory of Current Research on Higher Education,* published two years ago for the Carnegie Commission on the Future of Higher Education. It cataloged 921 research projects dealing with higher education, the first time a systematic compilation of the field had been attempted apart from the occasional summaries of the American Educational Research Association and the infrequent educational encyclopedias. And even the Heckman-Martin inventory was a one-shot project, only inadequately maintained by the ERIC Clearinghouse on Higher Education since then.

In the United States, the best model of a metainformation center in any field is the National Referral Center for Science and Technology, run by the Division of Science and Technology of the Library of Congress and located on the fifth floor of the Library Annex in Washington. Its aim is to be a single place to which anyone with an interest in science and technology may turn for advice on where and how to obtain information on specific topics. Thus it is a people bank: a referral center that directs inquirers to over eight thousand experts in other organizations throughout the country who have agreed to be available to help. Thus the center can direct a person interested in finding out the facts about the tides in Boston Harbor to a specialist in the Tides and Currents Branch of the Coast and Geodetic Survey. It might direct an inquirer about termite attractants to a chemist in the Forest Products Laboratory of the Department of Agriculture. And it could alert someone interested in the reclamation of diamond power from sludge to four sources including the Industrial Diamond Association of America.

Opened in 1963 with National Science Foundation support, the center presently operates on a budget of approximately $150,000 a year through Library of Congress appropriations. Staffed by ten people, it is getting between fifty and sixty requests a week from international agencies, scientists, librarians, and an occasional grade-school student. It tries for a five-day turn-around time in supplying the names, addresses, and telephone numbers of expert organizations, institutions, and individuals in the field of inquiry. In short, it is a model *referral* center for bringing people together. It is not a *reference* center that directs people to books, journal articles, and bibliographic references: instead it refers bibliographic inquiries to other sources of information.

For *Information*	*National Referral Center for* *Science and Technology* *Library of Congress* *Washington, D.C. 20540* *For referral service:* *(202) 426–5670* *For general inquiries:* *(202) 426–5687*

We suggest that the community of higher education needs some similar service: more responsive, more comprehensive, more authoritative than any of its present loci of information. Today in higher education no organization adequately serves this metainformation need. Instead certain individuals informally play this role—prominent among them being particular foundation officers, association executives, and scholars, with Arthur Adams, Fred Bolman, W. H.

Information Centers

Cowley, Lewis Mayhew, Marshall Robinson, Robert Wert, Logan Wilson, and Paul Woodring as examples. Periodically, proposals have been made for opening up this informal network of individual contacts by organizing some type of referral service within higher education, but most of these plans have come to naught. The Fund for the Advancement of Education considered the idea; S. Avery Raube at the National Industrial Conference Board has tried to implement it; and Robert Hind at the Educational Development Center, John A. Hrones at Case Western Reserve, and Edward Pomeroy at the American Association of Colleges for Teacher Education have each advocated the creation of agencies that would have met at least some of the need, but so far to no avail.

The one attempt that came closest of all to serving this function blossomed nearly fifteen years ago and then withered: the Office of Statistical Information and Research of the American Council on Education. Stemming from a study by Richard Sullivan of the need for access to statistical information about students, OSIR came into being in 1956 to fill this void. Under Elmer West's direction it sought to bring order into the morass of higher education statistics and definitions, stimulated the development of the field of institutional research, rode herd on the proliferation of questionnaires within higher education, and consolidated existing data into the ACE *Fact Book on Higher Education.* It came close to being a metainformation agency, but with changes in the orientation of the Council, it was superseded by Alexander Astin's research program and its activities have languished. As a consequence, the academic community lacks a comprehensive information center about itself.

Information Services for Academic Administration

PRESENT CENTERS

Currently, apart from knowledgeable individuals scattered throughout the academic enterprise, these are the major centers of information about higher education that are prepared to handle inquiries:

General Information Centers

THE INFORMATION OFFICERS OF THE INSTITUTIONAL
ASSOCIATIONS

Out of over four hundred associations concerned with higher education only a hundred maintain Washington offices, and only a handful of these have staff members specifically assigned to handle requests for information. At the American Council on Education, Frank Skinner, its information officer and editor of *Higher Education and National Affairs,* has the responsibility for answering inquiries or routing them to other members of the staff. Garven Hudgins does the same thing at the National Association of State Universities and Land-Grant Colleges, as does William Harper at the American Association of Junior Colleges. These offices have tended to be news and public-relations oriented, however, rather than research based. They rely for much of their own information on press releases by the thousands from their constituent institutions, but they do respond to inquiries ranging from facts about student-faculty ratios, faculty tenure policies, and student codes, to "Who's built a library recently in the four million dollar range?—because that's how much we've got on hand to spend."

Information Centers

Under pressure, the major Washington-based higher education associations are trying to devise a system of information collection and distribution that would rely less heavily on press releases. So far it is more plan than reality. The most encouraging step thus far has been the creation by the American Council on Education of the beginnings of a coordinated library for the associations, located in the National Center for Higher Education, professionally staffed, and reference oriented.

Information Services for Academic Administration

For Information

Mrs. Carolyn C. Leopold
National Center for Higher
Education Library
Suite 640
One Dupont Circle
Washington, D.C. 20036
(202) 833–4690

OFFICE OF RESEARCH, AMERICAN COUNCIL ON EDUCATION

Alexander W. Astin's workshop, built in 1965 on the ruins of the ACE Office of Statistical Information and Research, makes its computer files available to qualified researchers. Adolescent psychologists, organizational theorists, and institutional research specialists can find much data in them, but probably not the practicing administrator. The office operates on a five hundred thousand dollar budget, with roughly half of the total coming from federal sources and the rest from ACE dues and foundation grants. It has two major types of data available for analysis:

First, facts on institutional characteristics of colleges and universities. Data from the institutional exhibits in the ACE directories of colleges and universities, from the annual HEGIS surveys of the United States Office of Education, and the CASE data of the National Science Foundation on federal support to colleges for 1963–1966, all have been cleaned up by the staff of the Office of Research to reduce their incompatibility and then entered on computer tape. From analyzing these data, you could learn the extent of various calendar plans, such as semesters versus quarters, requirements about attending chapel, institutional median scores on SAT and ACT tests, the number of degrees conferred, and the like. (For details, see the booklet by J. A. Creager and C. L. Sell,

"The Institutional Domain of Higher Education: A Characteristic File for Research," *ACE Research Reports,* 1969, *4* [6].)

Second, data on students at selected institutions, stemming from the Cooperative Institutional Research Program of the Council. At four hundred colleges and universities each year, over three hundred thousand freshmen complete the ACE Student Information Form on their attitudes, activities, and characteristics; and periodic resurveys are run on them later. Data range from the number of one's close friends to the frequency of dating, taking sleeping pills, and being late to class, and an over-all evaluation on a five-point scale of their institution. (For details, see A. E. Bayer et al., "User's Manual: ACE Higher Education Data Bank," *ACE Research Reports,* 1969, *4* [1].) Institutions other than the sample four hundred can use the Student Information Form with permission and at their own expense.

For *Information*	*Alexander W. Astin* *Office of Research* *American Council on Education* *One Dupont Circle* *Washington, D.C. 20036* *(202) 833–4754*

UNITED STATES OFFICE OF EDUCATION

When Alexander M. Mood came from the Department of Defense to organize the National Center for Educational Statistics at the Office of Education, he and Jack Smith of the computer division of the office wanted the center to operate an information service with direct lines to the fifty state departments of education, so that state officials could dial Washington and ask questions about Office of Education data.

They got as far as obtaining some consoles for the teletype system, but, as Mood reminisces, "the office regarded it as some sort of Buck Rogers thing," and so the center remains a repository of vast amounts of unused data.

The office staff is obliging in trying to answer inquiries, once you know whom to reach for the information you need; but it is not geared to operate as an inquiry center. In fact, it has been known to refer questions about its own data to the American Council on Education. Whether the Office of Education will ever be able to respond to the needs of colleges and universities is doubtful. Certainly it will not do so as long as it considers its prime clientele for its statistics to be the federal government and not the educational community. At the moment, the best source of college and university information within the Office of Education is William Gescheider's office in the Bureau of Higher Education, with hopeful developments occurring within the National Center for Educational Communication. But in general the Office of Education cannot be considered an inquiry service of much use: it continues to try to meet the need for information through long-delayed publications.

For Information

William Gescheider
Chief of the Planning, Evaluation, and Reports Staff
Bureau of Higher Education
United States Office of Education
Regional Office Building
Seventh and D, S.W.
Washington, D.C. 20202
(202) 962–3116

Information Centers

ERIC (EDUCATIONAL RESOURCES AND INFORMATION CENTER)
CLEARINGHOUSES

Four of the nineteen ERIC clearinghouses that have
been established by the Office of Education are particularly
relevant to higher education: those on junior colleges, teacher
education, counseling and personnel services, and higher education at large. But the ERIC clearinghouses have been established to publicize documents and literature in education, and
have not been encouraged by the Office of Education to handle
requests for information other than to provide the accession
numbers of documents relevant to the inquiry. Some clearinghouses, the one on junior colleges among them, provide extensive assistance to inquirers. Others do not. Instead, they
undertake three primary tasks.

First, they prepare abstracts of fugitive literature such
as committee reports, papers read at professional meetings, and
local, state, or regional agency documents that might not
otherwise reach national attention. About fifty of these abstracts from each clearinghouse appear each month in *Research in Education,* the bibliographic journal of the Office of
Education listed in Chapter Six. Second, they draft bibliographic citations on relevant articles that appear in periodicals
for listing in the cumulative journal, *Current Index to Journals
in Education,* also described in Chapter Six. Third, they publish compendia on research and syntheses of developments in
the area of concern of the clearinghouse. For example, the
ERIC Clearinghouse on Higher Education has printed an
annotated bibliography on *Student Participation in Academic
Governance* by L. H. Robinson and J. D. Shoenfeld, and
compendia of developments in academic governance and the
preparation of college teachers (*Compendium Series of Current Research, Programs, and Proposals,* Number One: Governance, Number Two: Preparing College Teachers, by Carol

Schulman). Among its new series of integrative reviews and syntheses of knowledge are Wilbert McKeachie's *Research on College Teaching: A Review* and Jonathan R. Warren's *College Grading Practices: An Overview*.

	Carl Lange, Director
	ERIC Clearinghouse on Higher
	Education
	Suite 630
	One Dupont Circle
	Washington, D.C. 20036
	(202) 296–2597
	Gary Walz, Director
	ERIC Clearinghouse on
	Counseling and Personnel Services
	Third Floor, 611 Church Street
	Ann Arbor, Michigan 48104
	(313) 764–9492
For	*Arthur M. Cohen, Director*
Information	*ERIC Clearinghouse for Junior*
	College Information
	Room 96, Powell Library
	University of California at Los
	Angeles
	Los Angeles, California 90024
	(213) 825–3931
	Joel Burdin, Director
	ERIC Clearinghouse on Teacher
	Education
	Suite 616
	One Dupont Circle
	Washington, D.C. 20036
	(202) 293–7280

In short, although some ERIC clearinghouses serve as reference or information centers, their central purpose is the mass dissemination of bibliographic information. Inquiries about the topics covered by any of the clearinghouses or about the literature on these topics can as well be directed to Charles Haughey's office in the new Educational Reference Center within the Office of Education.

For Information

Charles Haughey, Educational Reference Center, Division of Information Resources, National Center for Educational Communication United States Office of Education 400 Maryland Avenue, S.W. Washington, D.C. 20202 (202) 962–7721

CENTER FOR RESEARCH AND DEVELOPMENT IN HIGHER EDUCATION, UNIVERSITY OF CALIFORNIA, BERKELEY

The Berkeley R&D center is the one university center on higher education that attempts in a formal way to serve as an information center. Operating on a million dollar annual budget, nearly all of which comes from Office of Education funds, the center is moving into dissemination activities after having organized the most broad-ranging research program on higher education in the country. Thus the center has been running a series of four invitational workshops with support from the Danforth Foundation in order to bring researchers and practitioners together to consider the implications from research in state-wide planning, innovation through cluster colleges, graduate education, and academic governance. In the future it hopes to assist groups of colleges to resolve problems of internal governance and to develop cooperative institutional research among themselves.

The Office of Education discourages the center from aiding only selected institutions instead of serving all of them; and so far, the center has been able to respond to individual inquiries for information primarily by referring to its own research and not to other sources.

In 1968 the Danforth Foundation was on the verge of underwriting the center with up to a million dollars a year to permit it to develop its referral services as well as to publish monthly critiques on particular topics and to hold regional conferences to make better use of research findings in improving educational practice. Danforth backed down because of previous over-commitments and a desire to assist in urban affairs after the death of Martin Luther King, but the center still hopes to move into these activities. It has more potential for doing so than any other university center on higher education, but so far it has not been able to do so on a large scale.

For Information	*Leland L. Medsker, Director* *Center for Research and* *Development in Higher Education* *University of California, Berkeley* *Berkeley, California 94720* *(415) 642–5040*

THE ACADEMY FOR EDUCATIONAL DEVELOPMENT

A nonprofit consulting firm with offices in New York and Washington, the academy is currently setting up a new division of higher education management financed by several grants (including a major one from Kellogg) amounting to over a million dollars. The new division will provide management information to central administrators of colleges and universities and will have access to the resources of the Conference Board (formerly the National Industrial Conference Board) which provides similar help to business and industrial executives. It plans research, publications in various media, conferences, seminars, and possibly a telephonic information service.

For Information	*Alvin C. Eurich, Director* *Higher Education Management Division* *Academy for Educational Development* *437 Madison Avenue* *New York, New York 10022* *(212) 758–5454*

Specialized Information Centers

Several other organizations have either begun to serve as information centers in specific fields within higher education or are planning to do so. Among them are these:

EDUCATIONAL TESTING SERVICE

ETS is planning to become a national information center on students. It is currently organizing an ERIC Clearinghouse on Evaluation, and already it can not only indicate to a college administrator the standing of his institution with respect to national norms on any ETS test, but it can also compare his institution with a tailor-made reference group of other institutions that he may choose—the only restriction being that the reference group must include at least ten institutions. The directors of each of the separate ETS testing programs are in charge of this new service and can be contacted directly about it.

| For Information | *Educational Testing Service*
Princeton, New Jersey 08540
(609) 921–9000 |

THE INTERUNIVERSITY COMMUNICATIONS COUNCIL (EDUCOM)

This is a consortium of a hundred colleges and universities interested in computer communication which has now moved to the ETS campus at Princeton, with Henry Chauncey assuming its presidency. Chauncey wants to make EDUCOM, in cooperation with ETS, into the national resource center for information and assistance on computers and communications for higher education. With NSF and Office of Education funds, EDUCOM has organized an Educational Information Network to share computer programs and other software systems. The network lists computer programs available at member institutions that can be used by other researchers if they want to send their data there to be run.

| For Information | *Henry Chauncey, President*
Interuniversity Communications
Council, Inc. (EDUCOM)
Post Office Box 364
Rosedale Road
Princeton, New Jersey 08540
(609) 921–7575 |

THE EDUCATION COMMISSION OF THE STATES

With forty-two states and territories now as members, ECS hopes to become the information gathering and dis-

136

semination center regarding interstate, state-federal, and state-institution concerns in higher education, both by conducting its own research and by developing access to centers of information elsewhere. It has brought Richard Millard, the former dean of liberal arts at Boston University and later chancellor of the Massachusetts system of higher education, to Denver as its director of higher education. Despite continued suspicion from some educators about the extension of its political power, the commission is still trying to bring educators and politicians together, and is working with state education officials and state-wide boards of higher education both individually and through their own associations by means of its Council of Higher Education Agencies (page 37).

	Richard Millard, Director of
	Higher Education
	Education Commission of the
For	*States*
Information	*822 Lincoln Tower*
	1860 Lincoln Street
	Denver, Colorado 80203
	(303) 255–3631

THE NATIONAL COMMISSION ON ACCREDITING

Organized by the colleges and universities of the country to bring some order into the accrediting field and to serve in effect as their accreditor of accrediting agencies, NCA responds to inquiries about accreditation and refers appropriate questions to the six regional accrediting associations or any of the specialized accrediting agencies in the thirty-six professional fields recognized for accreditation by the commission.

Information Services for Academic Administration

	Frank G. Dickey
	Executive Director
	National Commission on
For	Accrediting
Information	One Dupont Circle
	Washington, D.C. 20036
	(202) 296–4196

THE NATIONAL STUDENT ASSOCIATION

With Ford Foundation support, NSA has organized an active series of study and dissemination projects on topics including student legal rights, drugs, women's studies, and academic reform. Its Center for Educational Reform is serving as a clearinghouse for information on educational experiments, and rather than waiting for a path to be beaten to its Washington, D.C., door it dispatches its ELF Bus (for Educational Liberation Front), loaded with resource materials, for stops at interested campuses throughout the country.

	Center for Educational Reform
	National Student Association
For	*2115 S Street, N.W.*
Information	*Washington, D.C. 20008*
	(202) 387–5100

THE KANSAS CITY REGIONAL COUNCIL FOR HIGHER EDUCATION

This consortium serves voluntarily as a clearinghouse and referral center to information on the academic consortium movement, of which KCRCHE itself with its eighteen cooperating institutions is among the most active examples. Some sixty other full-scale academic consortia are listed in KCRCHE's current directory, ranging from close-knit local amalgams like the Claremont Colleges to national cooperative associations like the Union for Experimenting Colleges and Universities, with hundreds of more limited interinstitutional

138

ventures under way as well. KCRCHE refers specific inquiries to the most appropriate of them and tries to keep posted about new ones.

For *Information*	*Lewis D. Patterson* *Director of Program Development* *Kansas City Regional Council* *for Higher Education* *Suite 320* *4901 Main Street* *Kansas City, Missouri 64112* *(816) 561–6693*

JUSTIN MORRILL COLLEGE

Located at Michigan State University, this college has agreed to serve as a clearinghouse for information and contacts among cluster colleges, of which at least fifty are now in operation around the country. The clearinghouse is beginning informally with financial support from other cluster colleges and with the hope of foundation support to permit it to respond to inquiries, maintain a central repository of information on cluster colleges, assist in convening conferences, and organize a file of vacancies and of faculty members interested in teaching in cluster colleges.

For *Information*	*Milton Powell* *Justin Morrill College* *Michigan State University* *East Lansing, Michigan 48823* *(517) 353–1658 or 353–4344*

THE CENTER FOR THE STUDY OF EVALUATION

Located at the University of California at Los Angeles, one of eight educational research and development centers funded by the Office of Education, the CSE is developing a variety of tests and measures for institutions to use in evaluating their effectiveness and is working with some ninety colleges and universities in trying out these instruments. It can respond to inquiries regarding ways to improve the evaluation of educational programs and educational institutions.

For Information	*C. Robert Pace* *Higher Education Evaluation Project, Center for the Study of Evaluation* *320 Moore Hall* *University of California at Los Angeles* *Los Angeles, California 90024* *(213) 825–2621*

THE NATIONAL ASSOCIATION OF COLLEGE AND UNIVERSITY BUSINESS OFFICERS

NACUBO aims at being the information center for fiscal and business problems of higher education, in addition to expanding its conference and publication activities.

For Information	*D. F. Finn* *Executive Vice President* *National Association of College and University Business Officers* *One Dupont Circle* *Washington, D.C. 20036* *(202) 296–2346*

THE INTERNATIONAL COUNCIL FOR EDUCATIONAL DEVELOPMENT

Formerly Education and World Affairs, this council set up a data bank on the nearly 2,200 international programs operated by some five hundred American colleges and universities, and plans to update its information on these programs annually.

	International Council for
For	Educational Development
Information	522 Fifth Avenue
	New York, New York 10036
	(212) 867-9450

THE ASSOCIATION OF GOVERNING BOARDS

Now representing 315 boards of trustees, the association hopes to organize a study center and a clearinghouse for research on academic governance as part of its on-going operations.

	J. L. Zwingle
	Executive Vice-President
For	*Association of Governing Boards*
Information	*of Universities and Colleges*
	One Dupont Circle
	Washington, D.C. 20036
	(202) 296-8400

EDITORIAL PROJECTS FOR EDUCATION

EPE is considering expanding its activities as an information center, since it already receives numerous calls for information as a result of articles in its *Chronicle of Higher Education,* its *15 Minute Report,* and its two series of magazine inserts.

	Corbin Gwaltney
	Executive Director
For	*Editorial Projects for Education*
Information	*1717 Massachusetts Avenue, N.W.*
	Washington, D.C. 20036
	(202) 667-3344

Information Services for Academic Administration

Beyond these national centers, some information can be obtained at the regional and state level through such organizations as the regional accrediting associations, the three regional interstate agencies—the New England Board of Higher Education, the Southern Regional Education Board, and the Western Interstate Commission for Higher Education—and state-wide associations and agencies.

CONCLUSIONS

Like everyone else, college and university officials prefer to have information available as they need it. They wish it to be on call. As a result they find few publications readily helpful and they attend association meetings primarily for the opportunity they provide for shop-talk. They seek access to credible sources of knowledge—either by calling a colleague at a neighboring institution, asking for the assistance of a consultant, or locating somebody somewhere who has some facts.

The producers of information for college administration probably are aware of this need, but they have not yet moved to meet it. The educational associations, government agencies, university centers of research, publishers, all continue to emphasize the production of print to the neglect of providing assistance. Some are considering expanding their reference and information services, but so far none is serving as a comprehensive information center for higher education that is open to everyone concerned about the operation of colleges and universities—trustees, faculty, students, alumni, and legislators, as well as administrators themselves; and there is no sign that without outside stimulus such a center will come into being. One should.

A variety of centers of information, knowledge, and scholarship about higher education is needed and is preferable to the centralizing of all information services for higher education in one organization or location. All of the information centers listed above, and more, are necessary. But *although information services should not be centralized, information about these services must be*. At least one center in the country should become a clearinghouse of information about information: a center more knowledgeable than any existing agency about the location of other sources of knowledge and expertise about higher education. A metainformation agency is necessary for the academic community just as the National Referral Center for Science and Technology already serves the scientific community.

Such an agency should supplement rather than supercede the present centers of information about higher education. It should not disturb already existing channels of communication. Instead it should help link present centers of information by operating as a scanning mechanism to keep track of *who* is knowledgeable about *what*. But the primary function of a people bank would be to direct inquiries to the most accurate sources of assistance on issues in higher education. It would respond rapidly to inquiries for information from people who do not now have access to existing resources, and would direct them to experts in their field of concern. It would aim at instant response to telephone questions and at response within one day to written queries. Often it would refer the inquirer to immediate sources of information, such as a standard reference book in his own library or nearby individuals, but if references or experts are not at hand, to people elsewhere who know the problem and its literature. Rather than giving advice about substantive issues such as adopting quarter or semester calendars or issuing injunctions, it would refer these questions about alternative courses of action to other advisors and agencies.

The major problem of a people bank is the validity of

its expertise, and hence it must be staffed by the individuals most broadly knowledgeable about higher education: individuals who are able to keep constantly in touch with the development of knowledge throughout the educational system. Its small central staff should be a team operation—a closely-knit group of four or five professionals, working with at least an equal number of skilled associates (including a reference librarian, who could receive calls, handle correspondence, and help categorize and file information). To keep on top of developments, the senior staff should spend a significant part of their time in scanning—telephoning, reading, and conversing. Only in this way could they avoid the weakness of many existing information services—reliance on second-hand information, publicity, and cronyism.

The people bank should be a national service, open weekdays from 9 Eastern time to 5 Pacific time, and it should aim at being equally accessible to individuals and institutions throughout the continental United States. But with this national orientation it could be located anywhere in the country. It might be operated by any of several existing organizations, agencies, or universities, but it should have liaison with all and be dominated by none. Agencies with other duties tend to treat response to inquiries as a secondary, low priority function. The goal of a people bank can best be achieved by an organization charged with this specific responsibility alone, and thus we advocate the creation of a tax-exempt, nonprofit corporation to operate it, with an advisory panel of representatives from interested organizations and agencies to recommend policy to this corporation.

As an experimental venture, the people bank should be underwritten initially by philanthropy. Depending on the results of its initial operation and on developments during the next several years within the federal government and the academic community, it might eventually receive support from government and academic sources as well as from user fees.

If such a metainformation center for higher education were now in operation, it could suggest that an institution interested in beginning a self study look at Dwight Ladd's findings about recent college and university self studies and contact knowledgeable individuals such as Ladd for specific information. It might refer an inquiry about state residency requirements for in-state tuition to Robert Carbone or another expert on the topic, one on the problems of consortia to Lewis Patterson in Kansas City, another on upper-division colleges to Robert Altman at WICHE, still another on grading practices to Jonathan Warren at the Western Regional Office of ETS, and others to similarly well-versed men and women, agencies and organizations throughout the country. In other words, this information center could make all of the present information resources for higher education more effective, available, responsive, and useful, by serving as a linchpin for the entire system.

Such a center could help cure the miasmic condition of information about higher education that now exists: where a serviceman writes from Vietnam to One Dupont Circle for information about college costs and wonders why he receives no reply; where a state university inquires in Washington about position papers on collective bargaining and receives no assistance; where a state department of education asks about symposia or institutes on higher education and obtains no help; and where individuals and committees in college after college want access to information about higher education which already exists and lies waiting for use but which by themselves they cannot find. The goal of such a center should be that of the information system at large: ready access through more media by more individuals at more institutions to more information. It should, in short, put people in touch with people, and need in touch with knowledge.

Directory:
Agencies and
Organizations

The following organizations and agencies are among those concerned with the administration and operation of colleges and universities. Not included are disciplinary and professional associations in specific academic fields, university departments of higher education, state associations or regional divisions of national associations, or consortia of institutions— all of which also provide information services for academic administration.

Directory: Agencies and Organizations

ACADEMY FOR EDUCATIONAL DE-
VELOPMENT
Higher Education Management
Division
437 Madison Avenue
New York, New York 10022
(212) 758-5454
Alvin Eurich, *Director*

AMERICAN ALUMNI COUNCIL
Suite 530
One Dupont circle
Washington, D.C. 20036
(202) 223-9505
Warren Gould, *President*

AMERICAN ASSOCIATION FOR HIGHER
EDUCATION
Suite 780
One Dupont Circle
Washington, D.C. 20036
(202) 293-6440
G. Kerry Smith, *Chief Executive
Officer*

AMERICAN ASSOCIATION OF COL-
LEGES FOR TEACHER EDUCA-
TION
Suite 610
One Dupont Circle
Washington, D.C. 20036
(202) 293-2450
Edward C. Pomeroy, *Executive
Secretary*

AMERICAN ASSOCIATION OF COL-
LEGIATE REGISTRARS AND
ADMISSIONS OFFICERS
Suite 330
One Dupont Circle
Washington, D.C. 20036
(202) 293-6230
J. Douglas Conner, *Executive
Secretary*

AMERICAN ASSOCIATION OF JUNIOR
COLLEGES
Suite 410
One Dupont Circle
Washington, D.C. 20036
(202) 293-7050
Edmund J. Gleazer, Jr., *Executive
Director*

AMERICAN ASSOCIATION OF STATE
COLLEGES AND UNIVERSITIES
Suite 700
One Dupont Circle
Washington, D.C. 20036
(202) 293-7070
Allen W. Ostar, *Executive Director*

AMERICAN ASSOCIATION OF UNI-
VERSITY ADMINISTRATORS
One Library Circle
Crosby Hall
Buffalo, New York 14214
(716) 831-5026
Andrew W. Holt, *Coordinator*

AMERICAN ASSOCIATION OF UNI-
VERSITY PROFESSORS
Suite 500
One Dupont Circle
Washington, D.C. 20036
(202) 466-8050
Bertram H. Davis, *General Sec-
retary*
Additional offices in New York,
New York, and San Fran-
cisco, California

AMERICAN COLLEGE HEALTH AS-
SOCIATION
2807 Central Street
Evanston, Illinois 60201
(312) 491-9775
James W. Dilley, *Executive Director*

Information Services for Academic Administration

AMERICAN COLLEGE PERSONNEL ASSOCIATION
1607 New Hampshire Avenue, N.W.
Washington, D.C., 20009
(202) 483–4633
Willis E. Dugan, *Executive Director*

AMERICAN COLLEGE PUBLIC RELATIONS ASSOCIATION
Suite 600
One Dupont Circle
Washington, D.C. 20036
(202) 293–6360
John W. Leslie, *Executive Vice President*

AMERICAN COLLEGE TESTING PROGRAM
Post Office Box 168
Iowa City, Iowa 52240
(319) 351–4470
Fred F. Harkleroad, *President*
Additional offices in Atlanta, Georgia; Boulder, Colorado; Bowling Green, Ohio; Grand Prairie, Texas; King of Prussia, Pennsylvania; Lubbock, Texas; Manhattan, Kansas; Northbrook, Illinois; Oklahoma City, Oklahoma; and Sacramento, California

AMERICAN CONFERENCE OF ACADEMIC DEANS
Dean of Faculty
Colby College
Waterville, Maine 04901
(207) 872–2791 or 873–1131
E. Parker Johnson, *Chairman*

AMERICAN COUNCIL OF LEARNED SOCIETIES
345 East Forty-Sixth Street
New York, New York 10017

(212) 986–7393
Frederick Burkhardt, *President*

AMERICAN COUNCIL ON EDUCATION
Suite 800
One Dupont Circle
Washington, D.C., 20036
(202) 833–4700
Logan Wilson, *President* 833–4711
Commission on Academic Affairs, W. Todd Furniss, *Director* 833–4720
Commission on Administrative Affairs 833–4774
Commission on Federal Relations, John F. Morse, *Director* 833–4736
Academic Administration Internship Program, Charles G. Dobbins, *Director* 833–4762
Institute for College and University Administrators, Charles F. Fisher, *Program Director* 833–4781
Office of Program Development, Richard Humphrey, *Director* 833–4776
Office of Research, Alexander W. Astin, *Director* 833–4754
Office of Urban Affairs, Martin D. Jenkins, *Director* 833–4658

AMERICAN EDUCATIONAL RESEARCH ASSOCIATION
1126 Sixteenth Street, N.W.
Washington, D.C. 20036
(202) 223–9485
Richard A. Dershimer, *Executive Officer*

AMERICAN FEDERATION OF TEACHERS
1012 Fourteenth Street, N.W.
Washington, D.C. 20005
(202) 737–6141
Roy Moyer, *Executive Director*

148

Directory: Agencies and Organizations

AMERICAN MANAGEMENT ASSOCIA-
TION
135 West Fiftieth Street
New York, New York 10019
(212) 586–8100
Donald G. Mitchell, *Chief Executive Officer*

ASSOCIATION FOR COMPUTING MA-
CHINERY
College Consulting Service
Post Office Box 9046
Salt Lake City, Utah 84108
(801) 322–4166
William A. Viavant, *Director*

ASSOCIATION FOR INSTITUTIONAL
RESEARCH
Educational Services
University of Alabama
Auburn, Alabama 36830
(205) 826–4000
Wilbur A. Tincher, *Secretary*

ASSOCIATION OF AMERICAN COL-
LEGES
1818 R Street, N.W.
Washington, D.C. 2009
(202) 265–3137
Frederic W. Ness, *President*

ASSOCIATION OF COLLEGE AND RE-
SEARCH LIBRARIES
50 East Huron Street
Chicago, Illinois 60611
(312) 944–6780
J. Donald Thomas, *Executive Secretary*

ASSOCIATION OF COLLEGE AND UNI-
VERSITY HOUSING OFFICERS
Director of University Housing
65 Hollister
University of Rochester
Rochester, New York 14627
(716) 275–4951
Chester J. Malanoski, *Secretary*

ASSOCIATION OF COLLEGE UNIONS
INTERNATIONAL
Box 7286
Stanford, California 94305
(415) 328–8017
Chester A. Berry, *Secretary*

ASSOCIATION OF GOVERNING BOARDS
OF UNIVERSITIES AND COL-
LEGES
Suite 720
One Dupont Circle
Washington, D.C. 20036
(202) 296–8400
J. L. Zwingle, *Executive Vice President*

ASSOCIATION OF PHYSICAL PLANT
ADMINISTRATORS OF UNI-
VERSITIES AND COLLEGES
Earlham College
Richmond, Indiana 47374
(317) 962–6561
John H. Sweitzer, *Secretary*

ASSOCIATION OF STUDENT GOVERN-
MENTS
1416 H Street, N.W.
Washington, D.C. 20036
(202) 347–4346
David Wanser, *Research Director*

ASSOCIATION OF UNIVERSITY ARCHI-
TECTS
M-131 Office of Campus Planning
Western Washington State College
Bellingham, Washington 98225
(206) 734–8800 extension 2383
Robert Aegerter, *Secretary*

ASSOCIATION OF UNIVERSITY EVE-
NING COLLEGES
1700 Asp Avenue
Univer.ity of Oklahoma
Norman, Oklahoma 73069
(405) 325–1021
Howell W. McGee, *Executive Secretary*

Information Services for Academic Administration

ASSOCIATION OF UNIVERSITY SUM-
MER SESSIONS
Dean of Summer Session
University of Hawaii
Honolulu, Hawaii 96822
(808) 944–7221
Shunzo Sakamaki, *Secretary*

ASSOCIATION OF URBAN UNIVER-
SITIES
Jacksonville University
Jacksonville, Florida 32211
(904) 744–3950
Robert Spiro, *Secretary*

CENTER FOR EDUCATIONAL REFORM
See National Student Association

CENTER FOR PLANNING AND DE-
VELOPMENT
American Management Associa-
tion, Inc.
Box 88
Hamilton, New York 13346
(315) 824–2000
Franklyn S. Barry, *Director*

CENTER FOR RESEARCH AND DE-
VELOPMENT IN HIGHER ED-
UCATION
University of California, Berkeley
1947 Center Street
Berkeley, California 94720
(415) 642–5040
Leland Medsker, *Director*

CENTER FOR RESEARCH ON LEARN-
ING AND TEACHING
University of Michigan
1315 Hill Street
Ann Arbor, Michigan 48104
(313) 764–0505
Stanford C. Ericksen, *Director*

CENTER FOR THE STUDY OF EVALU-
ATION
Graduate School of Education
145 Moore Hall

University of California, Los
Angeles
Los Angeles, California 90024
(213) 825–4711
C. Robert Pace, *Principal Investigator,* Higher Education Evaluation Project
(213) 825–2621

CENTER FOR THE STUDY OF HIGHER
EDUCATION
University of Michigan
1100 South University
Ann Arbor, Michigan 48104
(313) 764–9472
James I. Doi, *Director*

CHANGE MAGAZINE
59 East Fifty-Fourth Street
New York, New York 10022
(212) 753–8302
George W. Bonham, *Editor in
Chief*

*CHRONICLE OF HIGHER
EDUCATION*
See Editorial Projects for Educa-
tion

*COLLEGE AND UNIVERSITY
BUSINESS*
230 W. Monroe
Chicago, Illinois 60606
(312) 368–6500
Dennis Binning, *Editor in Chief*

COLLEGE ENTRANCE EXAMINATION
BOARD
475 Riverside Drive
New York, New York 10027
(212) 865–9500
Arland F. Christ-Janer, *President*
Additional offices in Atlanta,
Georgia; Austin, Texas;
Evanston, Illinois; Palo
Alto, California; Hato Rey,
Puerto Rico; and Washing-
ton, D.C.

150

Directory: Agencies and Organizations

COLLEGE STUDENT PERSONNEL IN-
STITUTE
165 East Tenth
Claremont, California 91711
(714) 624-3595
John L. Cowan, *Executive Director*

COOPERATIVE COLLEGE REGISTRY
Suite 10
One Dupont Circle
Washington, D.C. 20036
(202) 223-2807
Elizabeth S. Fisher, *Executive
Director*

COUNCIL FOR THE ADVANCEMENT
OF SMALL COLLEGES
Suite 750
One Dupont Circle
Washington, D.C. 20036
(202) 659-3795
Roger J. Voskuyl, *Executive Di-
rector*

COUNCIL OF GRADUATE SCHOOLS IN
THE UNITED STATES
Suite 740
One Dupont Circle
Washington, D.C. 20036
(202) 223-3791
Boyd Page, *President*

EDITORIAL PROJECTS FOR EDUCA-
TION
1717 Massachusetts Avenue, N.W.
Washington, D.C. 20036
(202) 667-3344
Corbin Gwaltney, *Executive Director*

EDUCATION COMMISSION OF THE
STATES
822 Lincoln Tower
1860 Lincoln Street
Denver, Colorado 80203

(303) 255-3631
Richard Millard, *Director of
Higher Education*

EDUCATIONAL RESOURCES AND IN-
FORMATION CENTER
See ERIC Clearinghouses

EDUCATIONAL TESTING SERVICE
Princeton, New Jersey 08540
(609) 921-9000
William Turnbull, *President*
Additional Offices in: Austin,
Texas; Berkeley, Califor-
nia; Durham, North Caro-
lina; Evanston, Illinois;
Los Angeles, California;
San Juan, Puerto Rico;
and Washington, D.C.

ERIC CLEARINGHOUSE FOR JUNIOR
COLLEGE INFORMATION
Room 96
Powell Library
University of California, Los
Angeles
Los Angeles, California 90024
(213) 825-3931
Arthur M. Cohen, *Director*

ERIC CLEARINGHOUSE ON COUN-
SELING AND PERSONNEL
SERVICES
Third Floor
611 Church Street
Ann Arbor, Michigan 48104
(313) 764-9492
Gary Walz, *Director*

ERIC CLEARINGHOUSE ON HIGHER
EDUCATION
Suite 630
One Dupont Circle
Washington, D.C. 20036
(202) 296-2597
Carl J. Lange, *Director*

Information Services for Academic Administration

ERIC CLEARINGHOUSE ON TEACHER
EDUCATION
Suite 616
One Dupont Circle
Washington, D.C. 20036
(202) 293–7280
Joel L. Burdin, *Director*

FEDERATION OF REGIONAL AC-
CREDITING COMMISSIONS OF
HIGHER EDUCATION
5454 South Shore Drive
Chicago, Illinois 60615
(312) 684–6220
Norman Burns, *Secretary*

FOUNDATION CENTER
444 Madison Avenue
New York, New York 10022
(212) 752–1433
Edna Brigham, *Acting President*

INSTITUTE FOR COLLEGE AND UNI-
VERSITY ADMINISTRATORS
See American Council on Educa-
tion

INSTITUTE FOR EDUCATIONAL MAN-
AGEMENT
Holyoke Center–625
1350 Massachusetts Avenue
Cambridge, Massachusetts 02138
(617) 547–1472
Winfield Knopf and John W.
Teele, *Codirectors*

INTERNATIONAL ASSOCIATION OF
COLLEGE AND UNIVERSITY
SECURITY DIRECTORS
University of Massachusetts
Amherst, Massachusetts 01002
(413) 545–0111
John Marchant, *President*

INTERNATIONAL COUNCIL FOR ED-
CATIONAL DEVELOPMENT
522 Fifth Avenue

New York, New York 10036
(212) 867–9450
James A. Perkins, *Chief Executive
Officer*

INTERUNIVERSITY COMMUNICA-
TIONS COUNCIL, INC. (EDU-
COM)
Post Office Box 364
Rosedale Road
Princeton, New Jersey 08540
(609) 921–7575
Henry Chauncey, *President*

MANAGEMENT INFORMATION SYS-
TEMS PROJECT
See Western Institute Commission
for Higher Education

MIDDLE STATES ASSOCIATION OF
COLLEGES AND SECONDARY
SCHOOLS
Commission on Higher Education
225 Broadway
New York, New York 10007
(212) 227–4250
Robert Kirkwood, *Executive Sec-
retary*

NATIONAL ASSOCIATION OF COLLEGE
AND UNIVERSITY ATTOR-
NEYS
625 Grove Street
Evanston, Illinois 60201
(312) 328–4440
Edwin D. Demrich, *President*

NATIONAL ASSOCIATION OF COLLEGE
AND UNIVERSITY BUSINESS
OFFICERS
Suite 510
One Dupont Circle
Washington, D.C. 20036
(202) 296–2346
D. Francis Finn, *Executive Vice
President*

152

Directory: Agencies and Organizations

NATIONAL ASSOCIATION OF STATE UNIVERSITIES AND LAND-GRANT COLLEGES
Suite 710
One Dupont Circle
Washington, D.C. 20036
(202) 293–7120
Ralph K. Huitt, *Executive Director*

NATIONAL ASSOCIATION OF STUDENT PERSONNEL ADMINISTRATORS
Post Office Box 751
Portland State University
Portland, Oregon 97207
(503) 229–4979
Channing Briggs, *Controller*

NATIONAL ASSOCIATION OF SUMMER SESSIONS
Dean of Educational Services and Summer Session
San Fernando Valley State College
Los Angeles, California 91324
(213) 349–1200
Willard Edwards, *President*

NATIONAL ASSOCIATION OF WOMEN DEANS AND COUNSELORS
1201 Sixteenth Street, N.W.
Washington, D.C. 20036
(202) 833–4256
Ann Rankin Harris, *Executive Director*

NATIONAL CATHOLIC EDUCATIONAL ASSOCIATION
Division of Higher Education
Suite 770
One Dupont Circle
Washington, D.C. 20036
(202) 293–5954
Rev. Clarence W. Friedman, *Executive Secretary*

NATIONAL CENTER FOR DISPUTE SETTLEMENT
Federal Bar Building West
1819 H Street, N.W.
Washington, D.C. 20006
(202) 659–5650
Willoughby Abner, *Director*

NATIONAL CENTER FOR HIGHER EDUCATION LIBRARY
Suite 640
One Dupont Circle
Washington, D.C. 20036
(202) 833–4690
Carolyn C. Leopold, *Librarian*

NATIONAL COMMISSION ON ACCREDITING
Suite 760
One Dupont Circle
Washington, D.C. 20036
(202) 296–4196
Frank G. Dickey, *Executive Director*

NATIONAL EDUCATION ASSOCIATION OF THE UNITED STATES
1201 Sixteenth Street, N.W.
Washington, D.C. 20036
(202) 833–4000
Samuel M. Lambert, *Executive Secretary*

NATIONAL SCIENCE FOUNDATION
1800 G Street, N.W.
Washington, D.C. 20550
George Arnstein, *Institution Relations Officer* (202) 632–7320

NATIONAL STUDENT ASSOCIATION
Center for Educational Reform
2115 S Street, N.W.
Washington, D.C. 20008
(202) 387–5100

153

William Anderson, Lawrence Magid, Douglas Moreton, Karen Moyer, and Karen Ohmans, *staff*

NATIONAL TRAINING LABORATORIES
Institute for Applied Behavioral Science
1201 Sixteenth Street, N.W.
Washington, D.C. 20036
(202) 833–4341
Richard D. Albertson, *Director, Center for Educational Studies*

NEW ENGLAND ASSOCIATION OF COLLEGES AND SECONDARY SCHOOLS
Commission on Institutions of Higher Education
50 Beacon Street
Boston, Massachusetts 02108
(617) 523–0972
Robert R. Ramsey, Jr., *Director of Evaluation*

NEW ENGLAND BOARD OF HIGHER EDUCATION
20 Walnut Street
Wellesley, Massachusetts 02181
(617) 235–8071
Alan D. Ferguson, *Executive Director*

NORTH CENTRAL ASSOCIATION OF COLLEGES AND SECONDARY SCHOOLS
Commission on Institutions of Higher Education
5454 South Shore Drive
Chicago, Illinios 60615
(312) 684–6220
Norman Burns, *Executive Secretary*

NORTHWEST ASSOCIATION OF SECONDARY AND HIGHER SCHOOLS
Commission on Higher Schools
3731 University Way, N.E., No. 104
Seattle, Washington 98105
(206) 543–0195
James F. Bemis, *Executive Director*

REGIONAL EDUCATION LABORATORY FOR THE CAROLINAS AND VIRGINIA
Mutual Plaza
Chapel Hill and Duke Streets
Durham, North Carolina 27701
(919) 688–8057
Everett H. Hopkins, *President*

SOCIAL SCIENCE RESEARCH COUNCIL
230 Park Avenue
New York, New York 10017
(212) 689–1623
Henry W. Riecken, *President*

SOCIETY FOR COLLEGE AND UNIVERSITY PLANNING
308 Low Memorial Library
Columbia University
New York, New York 10027
(212) 280–5018
John D. Telfer, *Executive Director*

SOUTHERN ASSOCIATION OF COLLEGES AND SCHOOLS
Commission on Colleges
795 Peachtree Street
Atlanta, Georgia 30308
(404) 875–8011
Gordon W. Sweet, *Executive Secretary*

SOUTHERN REGIONAL EDUCATION BOARD
130 Sixth Street, N.W.

Atlanta, Georgia 30313
(404) 875–9211
Winfred L. Godwin, *Director*

SYSTEMS RESEARCH GROUP
252 Bloor Street West
Toronto 5, Ontario, Canada
(416) 964–8411
Richard W. Judy, Jack B. Levine,
Stephen I. Centner, *Principals*
370 Lexington Avenue
New York, New York 10017
(212) 686–5378
Joseph Sweeney, Bruce Peason,
and William Wolfson,
Principals
Educational Systems Research
Group
1601 Connecticut Avenue, N.W.
Washington, D.C. 20036
John Caffrey, *Principal*

TEACHERS INSURANCE AND AN-
NUITY ASSOCIATION OF
AMERICA
730 Third Avenue
New York, New York 10017
(212) 697–7600
Thomas C. Edwards, *President*

UNITED STATES OFFICE OF EDUCA-
TION
400 Maryland Avenue S.W.
Washington, D.C. 20202
National Center for Educational
Communication
Lee G. Burchinal, *Director* (202)
962–6346

National Center for Educational
Statistics
Dorothy Gilford, *Director* (202)
963–5136
William Gescheider, *Chief of the
Planning, Evaluation, and
Reports staff, Bureau of
Higher Education*
(202) 962–3116

WESTERN ASSOCIATION OF SCHOOLS
AND COLLEGES
Accrediting Commission for Senior
Colleges and Universities
Mills College
Seminary Avenue and MacArthur
Boulevard
Oakland, California 95350
(415) 632–5000
Kay J. Anderson, *Executive Secre-
tary*
Accrediting Commission for Ju-
nior Colleges
Modesto Junior College
Modesto, California 95350
(209) 524–1451, extension 214
Henry D. Wiser, *Executive Secre-
tary*

WESTERN INTERSTATE COMMISSION
FOR HIGHER EDUCATION
Post Office Drawer P
Boulder, Colorado 80302
(303) 449–3333
Robert H. Kroepsch, *Director*
Planning and Management Sys-
tems Program
Benjamin Lawrence, *Director*

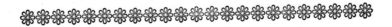

Index

Index

157

Index

sity Administrators, 46–47, 52–54, 65
Institute for College Development, 67
Institute for Educational Management, 54–55
Institute for the Study of Change in the Four-Year College, 46
Institutes and workshops, 16, 43–69; coordination, 47–49; cumulation, 50; evaluation, 51; financing, 46–47; involvement in, 50–51; present programs, 52–68; team orientation, 49–50
Institutional research, 16, 38–39, 128–129; Association for, 40–41, 42
Intelligence gathering, 20–29
Intercultural Education, 92
Interinstitutional cooperation, 36–37
International Council for Educational Development, 141
Internship programs, viii, 23
Interuniversity Communications Council, 40, 136
Inventory of Current Research on Higher Education, 123

J

Journal of Higher Education, The, 78, 85
Journals, 70, 78, 82–88
Junior College Journal, 73, 83
Junior colleges, 37, 64, 73, 83, 107, 126–127; publications, 73–74

K

Kansas City Regional Council for Higher Education, 138–139
Kellogg Foundation, 57–58, 134
Kettering Foundation, 87

L

Liberal Education, 78, 84–85

Liberal Studies, Special Committee on, 37
Lilly Endowment, 107, 115–116
Listening, 21–22

M

Management information systems, 25–26
Management Information Systems Project. *See* Planning and Management Systems Program
Management training, 114–115, 134–135; institutes, 54, 55, 65
Meetings, information sharing, 35–37, 44–45
Mellon Foundation, 53
Metainformation: characteristics, 122–125; described, 7–9; need for, 16–17, 74–75, 77, 98, 106, 122–125, 143–146

N

National Association of College and University Business Officers, 53, 65–66, 95–96, 140
National Association of State Universities and Land-Grant Colleges, 88, 126–127
National Center for Dispute Settlement, 110–111
National Center for Educational Statistics, 41–42
National Center for Higher Education, 127–128
National Commission on Accrediting, 137–138
National Institute of Mental Health, 38
National Referral Center for Science and Technology, 8, 123–124
National Science Foundation, 111
National Student Association, 91, 138
National Training Laboratory, 49, 56

Newsletters, 70, 75, 78, 88–93, 99

New York state consultation, 113–114

P

Periodicals, 70–99

Planning, 27–28; workshops on, 60–61, 65–66

Planning and Management Systems Program, 28–29, 56–57

Planning, programming, and budgeting, 27–28, 60–61

Polling, 24–25

Practical Law Institute, 49

Presidents Association, Inc., 62

Presidents' institutes and workshops, 34, 52–53, 54, 55, 57–58, 62, 63, 64, 65

Publications, 70–99; frequency of reading, 77–78; need for, 74–77; present, 77–99; recommendations for, 14; routing of, 71, 97–98

Q

Questionnaires, 24–25, 92

R

Recommendations, 31–32, 39–42, 47–51, 68–69, 98–99, 115–116, 122–123, 143–146

Records, usable, 25–26

Referral centers. *See* Metainformation

Report on Questionnaires, 92

Research and Development Centers, 140

Research, cooperative interinstitutional, 16, 38–39

Research in Education, 75, 80–81, 131

Research institutions, 36, 94

Research Reporter, 89

Resource Requirements Prediction Model, 28–29

Rockefeller Foundation, 37, 111

Rumor centers, 30–31

S

Saturday Review, 70, 72, 87–88

Science Information Exchange, 120–121

Sears-Roebuck grants, 53

"Selective Dissemination of Information," 97–98

Simulation, 28–29, 50, 60

Skills, use of available, 22–24

Sloan Foundation, 54, 111

"So They Say About Higher Education," 93

Society for College and University Planning, 66

Stern Foundation grants, 37

Student Information Form, 24, 129

Students, 21, 24, 56, 61, 129, 135

Syntheses, 76–77, 99, 131

Systems Research Group, 60–61

T

Teacher Education, American Association of Colleges for, 64

Team orientation, institutes, 49–50, 55, 56, 62, 67

Telephonic communication, 33–34, 103, 117–118

Travel, 34–35

Trustees: experience of, 22–23; information center, 141; institutes, 57–58, 62, 64, 65, 68; publications, 89–90

U

Union for Experimenting Colleges and Universities, 76–77

United States Office of Education, 68–69, 97, 129–130

W

Western Interstate Commission for Higher Education (WICHE), 23, 28–29, 56–57, 59, 66–67

Workshop on Liberal Arts Education, 67

Workshops, 16, 43–69, 133